Corporate
Dandelions

Corporate Dandelions

*How the Weed of
Bureaucracy Is Choking
American Companies—
and What You Can
Do to Uproot It*

Craig J. Cantoni

American Management Association

New York • Atlanta • Boston • Chicago • Kansas City • San Francisco • Washington, D.C.
Brussels • Toronto • Mexico City

This publication is designed to provide accurate and authoritative
information in regard to the subject matter covered. It is sold with
the understanding that the publisher is not engaged in rendering
legal, accounting, or other professional service. If legal advice or
other expert assistance is required, the services of a competent
professional person should be sought.

Library of Congress Cataloging-in-Publication Data

Cantoni, Craig J.
    Corporate dandelions : how the weed of bureaucracy is choking
American companies—and what you can do to uproot it / Craig J.
Cantoni.
        p.   cm.
    Includes bibliographical references and index.
    ISBN 0-8144-5119-5
    1. Bureaucracy—United States. 2. Organizational effectiveness.
3. Industrial productivity—United States. I. Title.
HD38.4.C36   1993
658—dc20   93-7663
                                                              CIP

Printing number

10   9   8   7   6   5   4   3   2   1

In Appreciation

This book is dedicated to **Kim,** whose support and understanding gave me the courage to leave the security, status, and high pay of corporate bureaucracy, and to **Christopher,** whose childhood innocence and wonder taught me what is important in life.

Contents

Preface

While not an autobiography—thank goodness—this book does have biographical elements in it, snapshots from my own twenty-year business career and, more important, from the careers of other business executives. These executives primarily held line positions in sales, operations, and manufacturing, where hard-working managers are forced to control the blight of bureaucracy affecting their own company while fighting the competition.

The primary goal of this book is to help managers stop the pernicious spread in their businesses of the weed known as bureaucracy, before it takes over and chokes the organizational flowers of creativity and risk-taking. Another goal is to help people trapped in boring bureaucratic jobs discover the joy of doing work that really matters, before they are spotted, like dandelions in a suburban lawn, and dealt with harshly by the popular weed-killer known as downsizing.

It would be easy for me to claim that I was never a corporate dandelion, that I never contributed to the spread of the bureaucratic weed. Easy but dishonest.

The painful fact is that, like other dandelions, I went along with the natural order of things out of self-interest, allowing the seeds of bureaucracy to propagate throughout my employers' organizations. And why not? Dandelions, after all, have become an accepted corporate flora, part of the natural business landscape.

But, as this book will show, organizational dandelions are not really natural flora at all. They are a human creation, with roots in the post–Industrial Revolution years of the early twentieth century. And having been created by humans, they can be controlled by humans. This book tells how.

This book is both lighthearted and serious, anecdotal and intellectual, pessimistic and optimistic, negative and positive, diagnostic and prescriptive. I hope the reader finds it both helpful and interesting.

Corporate Dandelions

Introduction

Buzzwords. In the mid-1980s it was "downsizing." At the end of the decade, "rightsizing." And now in the 1990s, "re-engineering." Oh yes, let's not forget "cultural change," "employee involvement," "total quality management," and "paradigm shift."

All of these buzzwords reflect techniques and concepts designed to help American business deal with the realities of global competition and diminished growth—that is, with lowered expectations. All reflect the new era of doing more with less, of being lean and mean, of focusing on quality. All are in response to the complacency and flab that had developed during the relatively easy post–World War II years of American economic dominance, which ran from 1946 to about 1973.

Many of these efforts have brought about a much-needed improvement in America's competitiveness, particularly in the manufacturing sector, where quality, productivity, and employee participation improved markedly in the 1980s. Unfortunately, some efforts were undertaken so stupidly and short-sightedly that they have resulted in the severing of the long-standing bond that used to keep employees and employers tied together with mutual trust and respect. Like a jilted spouse in an acrimonious divorce, employees are reluctant to ever again put their hearts and souls into a corporate marriage.

Worse yet, in spite of all the turmoil and pain of the last ten years, things are still pretty screwed up in today's organizations. After all the change, after all the billions spent on consultants, after all the upheaval, many companies are still dreadful places to work. Rigid and hierarchical, businesses still keep people in narrow organizational boxes, doing work that does not matter, pushing paper that no one wants, promulgating policies that no one needs, allowing little room for human creativity and fun. It is no surprise that so many employees admit to leaving their brains and ideas in their cars at the start of the workday, only to reinsert them like videocassettes when the day is over and it is time to go home.

Sadly, in too many cases downsizing efforts cut out people without a corresponding reduction in the amount of work, thus leaving fewer employees to handle the same workload, resulting in a dysfunctional level of stress among the work force. And the much-vaunted promises of productivity increases from information technology have not always materialized.

Even with all of the dislocation and cutbacks, it is estimated that more than one-half of the work force in American corporations are white-collar employees who work in administrative support positions and not in the core functions of sales, operations, or production.[1]

Accordingly, although manufacturing productivity (output per employee) increased 3.5 percent a year during the 1980s, it dropped markedly at the start of the 1990s. Productivity in services did not even come close, attaining an anemic 0.2 percent average increase in the decade; but even that weak performance fell during the closing years of the 1980s to a minus 0.5 percent.

Undoubtedly, as America pulls out of the recession in 1993, productivity will start to inch forward again, primarily due to the severe cutbacks in staff that normally occur during recessionary times, allowing firms to increase output as demand increases without immediately adding employees.

A 1992 study by the McKinsey Global Institute said that American service workers are the most productive in the world, surpassing even the Japanese and Germans.[2] Much of that productivity, however, is due to such measures as downsizing, wage and benefits cuts, and the use of part-time and contract employees, who normally do not receive medical coverage or other benefits. Although these measures allow companies to get more output per dollar of payroll, there is a social cost associated with them, a cost that our overseas trading partners are less willing to incur.

The real issue of productivity is white-collar overhead. A 1990 Boston University study showed that white-collar overhead was 26 percent of sales in the United States, versus 21 percent in Western Europe and 18 percent in Japan.[3] The 8 percent difference between the United States and Japan means that an average American company with $1 billion in revenues spends $80 million more on white-collar overhead than its Japanese counterpart. It is no surprise that the number one export from the New York harbor is scrap paper, and the number one import is manufactured goods from overseas.

The situation is not any better outside of the corporate world. Teachers now comprise less than 50 percent of the staff in many big-city school systems, being outstripped in numbers by administrative and service workers. Similarly, there were more senior officers in the military in 1990 than at the peak of World War II, when there were six times as many troops to command.[4] The Transit Authority of the bankrupt City of New York had twenty-eight vice-presidents in 1984 and sixty-eight in 1991—a 140 percent increase. And these numbers pale by comparison to the management featherbedding at the U.S. Department of Agriculture, where there is now one employee for every 16 farms, versus one for every 227,000 farms when the department was founded by Abraham Lincoln.[5]

What are all of these people doing? Why do organizations remain so top-heavy with administrative workers and so weighed down with overhead costs? Why, with all of the downsizing, is white-collar productivity so abysmal? Is it human nature or human behavior? Structure or process? Or is it systems, rewards, leadership, values, beliefs, measurements— or a combination of all these?

The answer lies in the much-misunderstood and maligned word *bureaucracy.*

Another buzzword? Another label for a new theory of the modern organization? Hardly. Bureaucracy has been with the human race since the start of civilization and the birth of the nation-state.

The modern version of bureaucracy was developed by the

French, thus the French roots of the word. In many respects, the caricature of the French governmental bureaucrat, surrounded by his rubber stamps and wearing his visor and arm band, is well-deserved. But the French certainly did not have a monopoly on governmental bureaucracy or bring it to its zenith. It reached full bloom, not with the French, but with the British Empire, where the expression "red tape" came into common usage from the red tape that was used to bind legal documents. The bureaucratic baton is now being handed off to the bloated United States government.

Bureaucracy in business organizations has its roots in a number of brilliant thinkers who, in the early 1900s, developed new theories of administration and control in response to the chaotic changes brought about by the Industrial Revolution.[6] These include the following: Henri Fayol (1841–1925), who put forward a universal theory of administration in *Administration Industrielle et Generale*, 1916; Harrington Emerson (1853–1931), who studied the Santa Fe Railroad and wrote *Efficiency As Basis for Operation and Wages* in 1900; and Frederick Taylor (1856–1915), the "Father of Scientific Management," who, in 1911, published *The Principles of Scientific Management*.

Perhaps the foremost theorist on bureaucracy was Max Weber (1864–1920), who wrote *The Theory of Social and Economic Organization*, which was translated into English by Gerth and Mills in 1946. Weber offered a precise technical definition and a rational model of bureaucracy. His writing led to the entrenched beliefs that bureaucracy and hierarchy are the most efficient forms of organization, that job duties should be officially prescribed and fixed, and that managers should use scientific methods and remain impersonal and unemotional.

Later management theorists, with backgrounds in psychology and sociology, began to apply behavioral science to organizations. From the 1930s through the 1960s, they put forth the idea that human work behavior is influenced by psychological and social needs, not just by structure and controls.*

*Luminaries like Elton Mayo, Mary Parker Follett, F. J. Roethlisberger, Kurt Lewin, Chester Barnard, Frederick Herzberg, Chris Argyris, and Rensis Likert are legends for their contributions to management thought.

At the same time, others began applying the disciplines of economics and statistics to business.* And still others were publishing books on management as a profession, including Herman Simon's *Administrative Behavior* (1947) and Peter Drucker's *Managing for Results* (1964).

In the 1960s, the field of organization development/change was started by such groundbreakers as Ed Schein, Warren Bennis, Eric Trist, Richard Walton, Herb Shepard, Warner Burke, Edith Seashore, Tony Petrella, and Marvin Weisbord. They looked at organizations as complex organisms influenced by a variety of interdependent variables, including teamwork, structure, rewards, systems, leadership, values, beliefs, and the external environment.

Present-day prophets include W. Edwards Deming, Tom Peters, Michael Hammer, Peter Senge, Rosabeth Moss-Kanter, and others too numerous to mention.

Over seventy years of brilliant management thinking have gone by since Max Weber defined bureaucracy. Why, then, are we still haunted by his ghost? Why are his tenets still practiced religiously? Why are corporations such stifling, bureaucratic, hierarchical places in which to work?

This book does not answer these questions by providing another complicated unified theory of the effective organization. Instead, it speaks in practical, easy-to-understand terms about how bureaucracy is one of the biggest and most overlooked impediments to individual and organizational effectiveness. The book is based on the belief that if nonproductive bureaucratic activity were to be transformed into revenue-generating activity, companies would not have to resort to downsizing or other draconian measures.

As the book will show, the dandelion is a perfect metaphor for bureaucracy because the weed and the organizational malady have so much in common. Both have deep roots, both

---

*One of the most notable was J. O. McKinsey, the founder of the international management consulting firm that carries his name, who developed budgetary techniques and applied them to Chicago retail giant Marshall Field and Company when he was chairman of the board. Another was W. A. Shewhart, who applied probability theory and statistics to quality control and other business problems.

pollinate easily, and both grow back if they are not removed, roots and all.

Given the French origins of modern bureaucracy, it is indeed fitting that the word *dandelion* also originates in French. Derived from *dent de lion*, the literal translation is "lion's tooth." And, as we shall see, the removal of corporate dandelions is just about as difficult—and dangerous—as the removal of a lion's tooth.

Through case studies, anecdotes, and interviews with business managers, this book will give true examples of how the seeds of bureaucracy take hold in organizations and how the weed can only be removed by the roots. Bureaucracy will be brought to life on the following pages, not through tedious theories, but through the experiences of real people—people who wanted to remain anonymous in case the bureaucrats in their organizations were to become agitated and attack them with whatever political means they have at their disposal to protect the status quo, just as the body's immune system protects itself by releasing white blood cells to attack a virus. The wishes of those contributors have been honored by masking dates, names, and places.

There are many examples of blatant bureaucracy on the following pages, but more subtle examples are also included, because bureaucracy is an insidious weed that takes root gradually and becomes well-entrenched before its harmful effects can be seen. It is as much a state of mind as a state of red tape and officialdom.

The reader will undoubtedly develop his or her own definition of bureaucracy by the end of the book, but some formal definitions might be helpful at the start.

Webster's Seventh New Collegiate Dictionary has two definitions of bureaucracy:

> **1.** government characterized by specialization of functions, adherence to fixed rules, and a hierarchy of authority; **2.** a system of administration marked by officialism, red tape, and proliferation.

Not bad. The definitions used in this book are just as simple. Bureaucracy is the following:

1. unnecessary activity that adds no value to the enterprise; **2.** a condition of cautiousness, conservatism, and entitlement that develops over time in mature, hierarchical organizations; **3.** a natural phenomenon that occurs when business managers lose touch with their customers and with the employees at the bottom of the organization who serve those customers.

The above definitions reflect the belief that bureaucracy is a much larger and more intractable problem than foot-thick policy manuals and unintelligible forms requiring ten approvals. Red tape is just a symptom of the problem, a physical manifestation of something else gone awry. This book focuses less on the symptoms and more on the something else—on the root causes of the problem.

How serious is the problem? Serious enough for John (Jack) F. Welch, Jr., the chairman of the General Electric Company, to say at the April 22, 1992, GE shareholder meeting: "We need to cultivate a visceral hatred of bureaucracy."

Part I of this book shares Jack Welch's opinion. Necessarily negative, it uses real companies and real people to demonstrate how bureaucracy seriously impairs organizational performance. Part II is much more positive. It focuses on the good things that can be done, and are being done, by companies to keep bureaucracy in check. Part III then takes the key points of Parts I and II and combines them into two brief but informative case studies. One case study describes how a multinational insurance company's attempt at decentralization backfired into a bureaucratic nightmare. The other describes a very successful effort of a well-known manufacturer at improving productivity by cutting through long-standing bureaucracy.

A word of caution before turning to Part I: Bureaucracy is so prevalent in corporate America that it would be highly unlikely for a reader not to find him- or herself in this book.

As the author can attest, facing the truth can be quite painful. But the alternative is to deny the truth and continue doing work that is of questionable value, robbing oneself of the opportunity to grow and develop, to come down from the stands to the action on the playing field, making oneself more valuable as an employee and, hence, more secure. Denial runs the risk of waking up one day stuck in a boring paper-pushing job removed from challenge and fun. Just as sad, it can lead to standing in the unemployment line with few marketable skills other than the ability to play an artificial bureaucratic game.

Notes

1. Richard Rosecrance, "Too Many Bosses, Too Few Workers," *The New York Times* (15 July 1990), p. F–11.
2. "Service Sector Productivity," McKinsey Global Institute study, Washington, D.C., October 1992.
3. The Boston University Study was referred to in: Thane Peterson, "Can Corporate America Get Out From Under Its Overhead?" *Business Week* (18 May 1992), p. 102.
4. Rosecrance, "Too Many Bosses, Too Few Workers," p. F–11.
5. George F. Will, "Whatever It Takes," *Newsweek* (23 March 1992), p. 72.
6. For an excellent history of management thought, see Joseph L. Massie, *Essentials of Management* (Englewood Cliffs, N.J.: Prentice-Hall, 1964).

I
Root Causes

1

Dandelion Seeds
The Genesis of Bureaucracy

The chances of getting hit by lightning are less than one in a million. That does not mean that people should defy the odds by standing on a hilltop in a thunderstorm with a metal umbrella in hand. What it means is that people can go about their normal lives without taking a lot of unnecessary precautions against the remote chance of getting hit by lightning.

Think of what would happen if the weather bureau said that the chances of getting hit by lightning were one in a hundred. All of a sudden, people would be reluctant to venture outdoors on any day but a sunny one. The makers of personal protective gear would earn millions by selling portable lightning rods that people could affix to the top of their heads. Smaller models would be developed for children and pets. People would become tentative about such simple chores as going to the grocery store and taking their dog for a walk.

Lightning Bolts in the Corporation

Farfetched? Not when it comes to corporate life. Rational executives in corporations many times act as if the odds of something dire happening were one in a hundred instead of one in a million, thus sowing the seeds of bureaucracy in the process.

Let's take a peek at a couple of actual employees on the job.

The corporate director of safety for a $1 billion industrial company was flushed with excitement as he interrupted the CEO at his desk first thing in the morning.

"Fred, did you see today's Wall Street Journal?*" he asked breathlessly.*

"No, what happened?" Fred answered impatiently, thinking that one of the company's plants had blown up.

"Company management of Illinois Wire* have been held criminally liable for the lead poisoning of their employees. They could face long jail terms and personal fines."

"What does that have to do with us?" the CEO responded with growing impatience.

"It means that you and other executives could be held criminally liable if employees were injured and you had known about unsafe operating practices but did nothing about them."

Bam! Like a two-by-four across the forehead, that got the attention of the CEO.

"Well, what do you suggest we do to protect ourselves?" Fred said.

"For starters, I'll need to draft a memo for your signature, issue a new policy for the safety manual, and get on an airplane to visit each of our facilities. Of course, I'll be talking to our general counsel and our outside consulting firm to see how we might be able to insulate ourselves from personal liability. It would also be a good idea for me to attend the upcoming Society of Safety Professionals seminar in Orlando. Don't worry. I'll keep you posted."

"Paul, thanks for staying on top of this. I'll give you all the support you need."

The safety director marched out of the CEO's office puffed up with pride like a strutting rooster, feeling important and part of the action. He headed straight for the company travel agent to make his travel plans.

Find the Dandelions

In looking for the dandelions in the above vignette, we could play the game found in the funny papers in which kids are asked to find certain items hidden in a cartoon drawing. But it would be unfair to ask you to play the game because, true to life, some of the dandelions are hidden from view. Let's strip away the camouflage.

---

*This was a real court case, but the name has been changed here.

The safety director in this actual conversation was a bright, aggressive high achiever, who at the age of 40 resented the fact that he was not always taken seriously by the general managers of the operating divisions. Feeling that he was stuck in safety for the rest of his career, he was always looking for ways to expand his influence and authority in the business. He saw the Illinois Wire case as a way to prove that he was on top of things and a man of action, a man who should be promoted to a higher position.

His needs for self-esteem, self-respect, and self-worth were all natural human needs. His intelligence, drive, and determination were all admirable traits. However, there was a large gap between the responsibilities of the position and the needs and traits of the incumbent. In typical human fashion, the safety director tried to close the gap by the only way he knew how—by expanding his activities to become more influential. He did not even think of finding a different job or career that would fit him better. No, it was much easier to stay put and enlarge the job to fit his needs, whether or not his needs matched those of the organization.

It was unfortunate for the organization that the safety director overreacted to the Illinois Wire case, whatever his motives. Like a lightning bolt, the chances of something similar happening to his employer were less than one in a million, but he forced his company to respond as if the odds were one in a hundred, generating unnecessary activity in the process (which is one definition of bureaucracy). In fact, the criminal liability decision in the Illinois Wire case was subsequently overturned on appeal, and the safety director's company was already in full compliance with all laws on workplace safety. But the safety director had already affixed lightning rods to everybody's head.

Cumulative Effect

As the previous example shows, the seeds of bureaucracy are sometimes too small to be spotted in the corporate landscape. The seeds sown by the safety director were neither obvious nor particularly harmful by themselves. However, when his seeds are combined with hundreds and thousands of other seemingly innocuous seeds, the cumulative effect over time is a weed-bound organization, one in which the dandelions have multiplied profusely.

The seed planted in the CEO's office, for example, soon resulted in a proliferation of dandelions in the form of unnecessary memos, policies, airplane tickets, and most important, an expenditure of management time in the divisions, where this valuable resource could have been directed outward at the competition instead of inward at useless activity. Inwardly focused activity is as harmful as a boxer who dances around the ring punching himself in the face instead of punching the competition.

What did the director's actions cost the company? A summary is given below:

Airfare to visit company facilities	$ 6,000
Attendance at Orlando seminar	2,000
Administrative costs of issuing policy	1,000
Advice from consulting firm	500
Wasted management time (estimate)	10,000
Total costs	$19,500

Was this a lot of money or a drop in the corporate bucket? To put it in perspective, the company could have taken out a full-page advertisement in a trade magazine for the same price. There is little doubt where a smaller, entrepreneurial company would have put the money. But being a large conglomerate, the safety director's company could treat twenty grand like Monopoly money. Sooner or later, though, such profligate spending adds up to real money, even for a big business.

Nipped in the Bud

The CEO in the safety director vignette could have nipped the growth of bureaucracy in the bud and given the safety director a valuable lesson in how *not* to succeed in his organization. All he had to do was ask these simple questions:

1. What exactly was the illegal activity done by the executives of Illinois Wire?
2. Do we conduct the same type of activity? If so, what is the quickest and cheapest way of stopping it? If not, why do we need to worry?
3. What are the odds of something like this happening to us? What are the costs and the benefits of eliminating all risk?

A Common Story

Is the story of the safety director an unusual one? Not at all. Check the in-boxes of staff specialists in any company and you will find a thick stack of ominous-sounding bulletins from consultants and law firms, spelling out in alarmist language how companies can get into legal trouble. Or attend a typical human resources association meeting, where a frequent guest speaker is an attorney dressed in an expensive suit who recites the typical litany of huge jury awards given to wronged employees. Of course, neither the speaker nor most of the meeting participants are really interested in reforming the system, because both parties gain from the slow strangulation of American business. Human resources people gain increased clout, staff, and pay in their organizations because of the fear of real and imagined lawsuits, and attorneys gain handsome fees from litigating the ever-increasing lawsuits.

The volume of self-serving, alarmist information bombarding organizations is like the firepower inflicted on Iraq during Desert Storm. After that kind of pounding, it is easy to surrender to the larger, bureaucratic forces at work in society and to forget how things used to be when America was preoccupied with producing instead of redistributing wealth.

Just one small example of the relentless pounding is shown below. It is taken from the brochure of a company selling a $250 annual subscription to a newsletter on employment law.

- Anita Hill & Clarence Thomas Hearings
- Sexual Harassment • Equal Pay
- Fetal Protection • Carpal Tunnel Syndrome

- Americans with Disabilities Act
- Civil Rights Act   • Title VII
- Glass Ceilings   • Employment at Will
- Age Discrimination   • Reverse Discrimination
- Unlawful Discharge   • Job Stress

Not understanding these laws
could seriously impact your
company **AND COST YOU YOUR JOB.**

Just think of it. For only $250 you can learn the law and save your job!

Iron Laws

Speaking of laws, many chapters in this book will end with a listing of laws—the iron laws of bureaucracy. Unlike most other laws, however, the iron laws of bureaucracy must be broken for the good of the corporate community. Later chapters tell how.

Here are the first three laws. They have their roots in the lightning bolt phenomenon, that is, the tendency of staff specialists, consultants, and lawyers to exaggerate the probability of risks for their own self-serving motives.

Iron Law #1

Staff employees with unfulfilled needs for status, recognition, and power will create bureaucracy to satisfy those needs.

Iron Law #2

Self-serving outside consultants will create bureacracy by selling unneeded services.

Iron Law #3

Bureaucracy takes over slowly, one small seed at a time, until the organization is so weed-bound that it loses sight of the competition.

The third iron law above was proved by the retail giant Macy's, which began 1992 in bankruptcy court. A weed-bound organization, it operated through a centralized system of inflexible controls and operating procedures that had taken root over time. Slow to change, it could not keep up with its nimble competitor, Nordstrom's, which operates with a two-sentence rule book:

Rule 1. Use your good judgment in all situations.
Rule 2. There will be no additional rules.

Nordstrom's understands that bureaucracy proliferates one rule at a time until the organization is so weighed down with unnecessary bureaucratic baggage that it goes from being a racehorse to a plow horse.

You have to wonder what kinds of organizations and leaders would let bureaucracy-generators like the safety director proceed unchecked. The question is answered in the next chapter.

2

Dandelion Genetics

Bureaucrats Begetting Bureaucrats

Survival of the fittest is a law of nature. It applies everywhere but the unnatural world of the American corporation, where the unfit not only survive but propagate prolifically.

Survival of the Unfit

Unfit does not mean unintelligent, lackluster, or passive. Rather, it means someone who has neither the experiences nor competencies to be a decisive leader. It means an administrator who manages through rules and regulations instead of personal power and charisma; someone who maintains the status quo instead of creating the disequilibrium needed for positive change.

Through some sort of reverse Darwinian process, unfit bureaucrats have risen to the top floors of too many of the Fortune 500 companies, where they have given birth to large staffs and slow-moving bureaucracies. The bureaucratic offspring of such leaders are as abundant as dandelions in an unmowed field—even in this age of downsizing and cutbacks in white-collar workers.

This is not to suggest that fit business leaders do not exist. To the contrary, there are many outstanding business leaders in corporate America, some of whom will be spotlighted in later chapters. Unlike their unfit peers, the fit leaders are prolific at producing profits instead of bureaucratic offspring. Just as the lean body of an Olympic athlete reflects his or her athletic prowess, the lean organization of a fit business leader reflects his or her leadership prowess.

Unfortunately, it is much easier to produce bureaucracy than profits. Take the true case of the bureaucratic CEO who was displeased by the overly generous raises being granted by his senior managers. Instead of confronting them and establishing his expectations, the CEO turned to his human resources vice-president for a solution, thus giving birth to bureaucracy.

And a solution was found by the vice-president. She implemented a cumbersome salary budgeting procedure, added more policies and approval levels to the compensation manual, started requiring monthly budget updates from managers, and hired a person to handle the additional paperwork. In the process, operating managers lost a little more authority to the corporate staff; accountability between line and staff became fuzzier; and more corporate energy was dissipated on internal bickering and politicking.

A more fertile example of bureaucratic procreation is the accounting department of a 40,000-employee organization that requires a written justification whenever someone wants to attend a seminar out of state. It seems that a senior executive once discovered that managers were allowing their employees to go on junkets to exotic locales.

Because of the executive's refusal to deal firmly with the poor judgment of the few, the judgment of the many is now second-guessed by a staff bureaucrat. As a result, general managers responsible for multimillion-dollar budgets can no longer approve a $1,000 seminar without encountering delay and red tape. In private conversations with these managers, their anger at being treated so childishly quickly bubbles to the surface. So consuming is their resentment, they want to talk about little else.

Corporate Staff Inbreeding

How did such organizational mutations begin in corporate America? There are a number of reasons.

One reason is the ascendancy of staff experts to the top of American business. Schooled in such technical disciplines as finance and law, the experts have spent most of their formative years in organizations as individual contributors, not gaining the leadership skills, business intuition, and self-confidence that come with running a line operation like manufacturing or sales and being held accountable for measurable results. Unpracticed in resolving conflicts and making tough decisions, the staff experts insulate themselves from the messiness and uncertainties of day-to-day operations by relying on other staff experts, on clones of themselves. Evolving from the ranks of corporate technicians, many are simply more comfortable with their immediate family of staff experts than with their distant relatives in the line operations.

It would be unfair and grossly inaccurate to characterize all corporate staff experts as bureaucrats. Obviously, the majority are performing valuable work in a nonbureaucratic manner and making important contributions to their businesses. It is alarming, though, how many organizations have allowed their staff functions to become bureaucratic and to overtake the entrepreneurs and risk-takers in number, pay, and status. Perhaps the best example is the downfall of General Motors, where bureaucratic inbreeding has almost killed off the entre-preneurial genes of the body-corporate.

The conventional wisdom is that the decline of General Motors was triggered by the car invasion of the Japanese. The conventional wisdom is wrong.

The decline really started when the staff-expert function of finance took over the company in 1958, with the ascendancy of one of its own to the chairmanship. From that point on until 1991, with a succession of finance people in top management positions, the company developed a finance culture—one in which making the numbers became the primary goal; one that put production volume ahead of quality, economies of scale ahead of marketing, cost-cutting ahead of creative design, bureaucracy ahead of tough decisions. Manufacturing lost its preeminence during those years, becoming an organizational backwater that no longer attracted the best and the brightest. In the process, GM lost its ability to manufacture quality automobiles. By the time of the Japanese invasion, the one-time giant was so overgrown with dandelions that it could not push the more innovative and aggressive invaders back into the sea.[1]

Years of evolution under financial management finally created the ultimate GM chairman in Roger Smith, who at the end of the last decade was in charge of a company that took almost three times as many hours per employee as Honda to produce an automobile, and twice as long to design a new car. It came as no surprise that Smith got a case of indigestion after acquiring the information company Electronic Data Systems and its entrepreneurial chairman, H. Ross Perot, who was later expelled from GM in a much-publicized buyout. Dandelions do not like weed-killers in their organizations.

A similar growth of dandelions occurred at Ford for about a quarter of a century, starting in the late 1950s with the new president Robert McNamara, who brought the specialists in quantitative analysis, the "Whiz Kids," into the company.[2] The number-crunching approach to management did not work at Ford, but that did not stop McNamara from using the same approach to run the Vietnam War as secretary of defense—with the same disastrous results.

One bureaucratic CEO of a large, diversified company is known to be so conflict-avoidant that whenever he is in a contentious meeting with aggressive managers, he starts pulling on his earlobes, stretching them about a half inch when things really get hot. Rather than take a stand and make a decision, he will pull and pull until the observer begins to think that he will turn into Dumbo the elephant. The ear-pulling is a precursor to the CEO's next habit: requesting more information and more studies as a way of putting off making a decision. And sure enough, his managers dutifully go off and get more information and conduct more studies, only to encounter more ear-pulling when it is time again for a decision. The process is repeated over and over, wasting valuable time and energy, until the managers realize that they have been had, that all their work had been going into a bureaucratic black hole never to be seen again. Major issues in that company have been left unaddressed for years, as evidenced by a return on equity that is half that of the competition.

Another weak CEO, desiring to be a consensus manager, will avoid making a decision if there is any disagreement among his subordinates. Usually, whenever he senses disagreement, he will turn to his managers and ask them to work out a solution among themselves. As a result, the company takes a year to make decisions that other companies can make in days or weeks, and the decisions are usually weak compromises. This particular CEO spent his formative years in corporate staff positions, never managing large numbers of people or being held accountable for bottom-line results.

Decisive, results-oriented executives under this type of indecisive management either learn to submerge their frustrations or leave for more supportive and fast-moving organizations.

Endangered Species

Are the above examples anomalies? Not really. A review of the career paths of the top officers of Fortune 500 companies reveals that 50 percent came from the corporate ranks of finance, legal, corporate development, strategic planning, or other staff functions. Richard Rosecrance, a professor of political science at the University of California at Los Angeles, provided the reasons for this high percentage in *The New York Times:*

> In all too many of our organizations, management specialties—not production and meeting the needs of the consumer—are the way to the top. More than half of the modern American corporation consists of workers uninvolved in operations or production work, an astounding fact. At the General Motors Corporation, 77.5 percent of all the work force is white collar and salaried, while only 22.5 percent are hourly blue-collar workers. At Mobil Oil, 61.5 percent of the staff is white collar; at General Electric, 60

percent; at Dupont, 57.1 percent; at International
Business Machines, 91.5 percent. (Because IBM does
much of its manufacturing overseas and most of its
strategic planning at home, this is not surprising.) At
Exxon, the figure is 43 percent; at Ford, 37 percent; at
AT&T, 42 percent; at Chrysler, 44.4 percent. *The ratio
in typical corporations in Japan is about one-sixth of the
American figure.*[3] [Emphasis added.]

Robert Hayes and William Abernathy of the Harvard Business School would have agreed with this assessment. In a 1980
Harvard Business Review article, they talked about the "new
management orthodoxy" that was responsible for financial and
legal skills replacing product, market, and manufacturing
know-how in the executive ranks.[4] The result is the false
concept of the professional manager; that is, someone who
does not need any specific industry or technological experience
as long as he understands financial controls, portfolio concepts, and market-driven strategies.

One of the reasons for the ascendancy of staff experts is
the changed nature of American society. An explosion of
government regulations and litigiousness has resulted in more
value being placed on the protectors of wealth instead of the
creators of wealth, on risk aversion instead of risk-taking.

Nothing better symbolizes a wealth-protection society than
the burgeoning legal profession, which is the real growth
industry in America. In 1975, there were less than 400,000
attorneys in the United States; by 1990, the number had grown
by 75 percent to 700,000. Projections indicate that there will be
900,000 attorneys in the year 2000.[5] That astounding number
just about equals the 850,000 wealth-producing manufacturing
jobs that were lost in the last decade.

There is one lawyer for every 335 Americans, compared to
one for every 9,000 Japanese. In America, the ratio of engineers
to attorneys is one-to-ten; in Japan, it is ten-to-one. On the
average, one lawsuit is filed for every ten adults in America,
resulting in an economic cost of $4,800 for every family.

The cost to corporate America is even more staggering.
From workers' compensation abuses to medical malpractice,

from environmental lawsuits to OSHA fines, from product liability awards to discrimination charges—businesses pick up the tab for damages, real or exaggerated. According to the federal Office of Management and Budget, the private sector spends five billion hours a year just filling out federal paperwork. Is it any wonder that companies are headed by caretakers instead of risk-takers? Another reason for the risk-adverse nature of the modern corporation is the ongoing replacement of leaders with bureaucrats.

How do bureaucrats and leaders differ? In many ways.

The differences will be addressed more completely in later chapters, but some discussion is warranted at this point since, in the context of this chapter, the slow extinction of leaders is another sign of the unnatural survival of the weak in the American corporation.

A bureaucrat is someone who maintains the status quo, even in the face of irrefutable evidence that the perpetuation of the status quo will lead to the decline of the enterprise. A bureaucrat views his or her job as balancing the competing interests in the organization, to be the internal diplomat who ensures harmony and resolves conflict on a win–win basis. A product of the system, a bureaucrat keeps the organization in equilibrium and maintains its traditions and ways of doing business.

Strong leaders, on the other hand, create controversy by changing the balance of power. They intentionally bring about needed change in organizations by disrupting the status quo. With personalities that thrive on risk-taking and contention, leaders take organizations where they need to go but do not want to go.

Inevitably, as strong leaders force an organization to go outside its comfort zone, they make the members of the organization uncomfortable. Consequently, such leaders are labeled with a lot of "too" words, as in too forceful, too opinionated, too abrupt, too controversial, too autocratic. One of the strongest leaders in American business, Jack Welch of General Electric, has been given the handle of "Neutron Jack" by those who think he is too callous in shedding under-performing businesses. (Coming from GE's strategic planning function,

Welch demonstrates that not all staff specialists are bureaucrats.)

John D. Rockefeller III talked about the hurdles facing leaders in *The Second American Revolution*:

> An organization is a system, with a logic of its own, and all the weight of tradition and inertia. The deck is stacked in favor of the tried and proven way of doing things and against the taking of risks and striking out in new directions.[6]

It is no accident, then, that the natural selection process in organizations ensures the survival of the tried and proven ways of doing things by installing bureaucrats at the top who will perpetuate the tried and proven way of doing things. The "We've always done it that way" excuse for not changing things is always blamed on low-level bureaucrats. But the real blame should be directed at senior managers, who are too sophisticated to say "We've always done it that way," but who send the same message in a more subtle and more powerful way.

Abraham Zaleznik, Professor of Leadership Emeritus at Harvard Business School, had these thoughts on the development of managers:

> Out of this conservatism and inertia, organizations provide succession to power through the development of managers rather than individual leaders. Ironically, this ethic fosters a bureaucratic culture in business, supposedly the last bastion protecting us from the encroachments and controls of bureaucracy in government and education.[7]

Organizations tend to stay in a state of bureaucratic equilibrium because the people in them prefer the status quo over change. It is only natural for employees to want the security of knowing that the organization's rules and norms, its standards of behavior and prescriptions for success, will not be turned topsy-turvy. Those who have been with the organization the longest and have risen to the top by learning how to succeed in the old system will be the most resistant to change, feeling that they have the most to lose by buying into an unproven and unknown new way of doing things. "We've always done it that way" is their creed.

On the surface, such people seem to be completely irrational, apparently operating under the mistaken belief that the future will be like the past as long as the lessons of the past continue to be followed indefinitely into the future. Even when faced with the rapid changes brought about by global competition and America's eroding dominance, they hold on to the past like a sinking sailboat chained to an anchor in a storm.

In actuality, there is nothing irrational about these people. What they are really saying is completely rational: "I'll be damned if I'm going to risk everything that I've worked so hard to get by doing things entirely different from the past. Prove to me that the new way is going to work, and that I'm going to be okay."

Of course, it is impossible to guarantee that sailing into unchartered waters is going to be a risk-free journey. A strong leader, therefore, has to have the courage of his or her convictions, the ability to get people to share a vision of the future, a need to be respected rather than liked, and a high tolerance for contention. These are not the characteristics of bureaucrats.

Let's return to General Motors to see the status quo in action.

The Ultimate Bureaucracy

In the mid-1970s, in spite of all the evidence to the contrary overseas, the largest, richest car company in the world continued to believe that it could not make money in small cars. And because it believed this, it indeed did not make money in small cars.

The fact is that to make money in small cars, General Motors would have had to turn the organization upside down. It would have had to change its relationship with labor unions, its relationship with suppliers, the design of its factories, the way executives got rewarded, the way the business was measured, and the way the business was structured. And to protect its market share, it would have had to do all of this in short order—in years instead of decades.

Educated in a large car system, the brains of the executives and labor leaders were wired to understand and have faith in only one thing: making large cars. Even if they had understood the importance of making small cars, a critical mass for blowing up the status quo could not develop because the scope of the changes overwhelmed the circuitry of the key decision makers. The changes also required the entrenched management to be superhuman and admit that their long-held beliefs about how to make cars were wrong.

Moreover, it would have been supernatural for the finance culture to produce a leader with the vision and conviction to incur the risks and wrath of a complete organizational transformation. Predictably, rather than take the risks of transforming the GM culture, the decision makers stuck to the status quo, preferring gradual change to radical change, preferring to have their market share slowly stolen away than to have their tried and proven ways of doing things turned topsy-turvy. The GM natural selection process was not about to allow a strong leader to evolve to the top until the organization started to bleed profusely and had no other choice.

Mort Meyerson, an ex-member of GM's executive committee, is quoted in *Managing on the Edge* on the status quo at the car company:

> General Motors has evolved a system which restricts subordinates from challenging the status quo. It's like the Manchu dynasty in the latter stages of its decay. And I mean *really* like the Manchu dynasty— including eunuchs. There have been a great many senior executives at General Motors who have had their balls cut off. And worse, they seem to have accepted their fate in order to play some residual role in the declining empire. . . .[8]

General Motors is only the tip of the iceberg. Bureaucratic leaders, wealth-protectors, and staff experts are quickly becoming the norm in American business. In fact, the scales have been tipped in favor of corporate staff for so long that it is considered normal for the bureaucrats at the plush corporate headquarters across the country to have more prestige, power, and pay than the strong leaders on the firing line—more than the leaders responsible for making products in factories, developing products in laboratories, and carrying sales bags into customers' offices. If professional baseball was run the same way, the scoreboard keepers and umpires would make more money and be more famous than the players on the field.

Just how far the balance has been tipped will become apparent in the two short stories in the next chapter. The true stories follow two employees on a typical day. One is a vice-president of information systems making a base salary of $140,000. The other is a manufacturing director earning a base salary of $90,000. The information systems vice-president is a bureaucrat, not because he holds a corporate staff position, but because of the way he operates in that position.

First, though, this chapter will end with the following iron laws of bureaucracy:

Iron Law #4

Bureaucratic organizations are the natural offspring of bureaucratic managers.

Iron Law #5

Bureaucratic managers are the natural offspring of bureaucratic organizations.

These laws are depressing because they suggest that bureaucracy is circular in nature, with no clear cause and effect, with no clear beginning or end. If bureaucracy is caused by bureaucratic managers, and if bureaucratic managers are created by bureaucracies, how can the cycle be broken? The question is answered more fully in Part II, which spells out how some companies ensure that bureaucrats do not make it to senior leadership positions.

Notes

1. See Richard Tanner Pascale, *Managing on the Edge* (New York: Touchstone, 1990), for a description of how the culture of General Motors changed from manufacturing to finance.
2. A fascinating description of the Whiz Kids at Ford is included in David Halberstam's *The Reckoning* (New York: William Morrow, 1986). Another insightful history of Ford is Robert Lacey's, *Ford, the Men and the Machine* (Boston: Little, Brown & Co., 1986).
3. Richard Rosecrance, "Too Many Bosses, Too Few Workers," *The New York Times* (15 July 1990), p. F–11.
4. Robert H. Hayes and William J. Abernathy, "Managing Our Way to Economic Decline," *Harvard Business Review* (July–August 1980), p. 67.
5. U.S. Bureau of Labor Statistics, *Federal Courts Study Committee Report* (1 July 1990).
6. John D. Rockefeller III, *The Second American Revolution* (New York: Harper and Row, 1973), p. 72.
7. Abraham Zaleznik, "Managers and Leaders: Are They Different?" *Harvard Business Review* (March–April 1992), p. 127.
8. Pascale, *Managing on the Edge*, p. 238.

3

Dandelion World
Land of Perks, Power, and Politics

Bayou, Texas. Just outside of Port Arthur/Beaumont near the Louisiana border. A ninety-minute drive east on Interstate 10 from the center of Houston.

Part of the Texas Gulf Coast industrial belt, it is a gritty area of oil refineries, resin plants, and shipping channels. The humid air is heavy with the odor of chemicals cooking and the unmistakable pungent smell of a paper mill. In a display of Texas arrogance, the highway sign outside of the Welcome Inn says that it is 767 miles to El Paso.

The Welcome Inn is a standard-issue roadside motel. The rooms are neither modern nor old, neither decorated nor bare. It provides the essentials: a bed, a shower, a TV. At $49 per night, the eclectic mix of truck drivers, cowboys, and business people aren't complaining, especially with the convenience of a honky tonk and coffee shop next door. What else would one need?

The general manager of the Polyresin Division of American Products International is holding a meeting in one of the conference rooms. It's been a long day. Half-eaten sandwiches and coffee cups filled with cigarette butts are scattered around the U-shaped table, intermingled with Coke cans and wads of paper. Dressed in casual clothes, the meeting participants have weary looks on their faces.

"No, these numbers aren't going to fly with corporate headquarters," the general manager is saying in a tired voice. "We promised 12 percent return on invested capital and that's what we're going to have to deliver."

The operations director couldn't restrain himself. "Dammit, Chris, we could make our numbers if we didn't have to pay $1 million in allocations to corporate for their so-called services. Hell, that's 3 percent of our revenue. And for what? They've been working for over a year on an inventory control system for us and we have nothing to show for it but a lot of wasted time and money. I could've bought my own software package and had it up-and-

running in half the time for half the cost. Now we're getting beat up by corporate finance for having too much money in inventory. Don't those guys up there talk to each other?''

"Jim, you're right," Chris answered calmly, "but let's not get into that again. Reality is reality, and the reality is that we can't do a damn thing about the allocations or slow service."

"Yeah, but as you know it's not just the money or service that's the problem," Jim responded with less anger and more resignation in his voice. "What's even more aggravating is how they resist any new ideas. Here we are trying to organize the plant into self-managing work teams, and that jerk in personnel is telling us that we can't deviate from the standard corporate appraisal form and pay system. Hell. . . ."

Beep, beep. The operations director's beeper interrupted his tirade.

The general manager turned to the operations director and said: "Jim, go ahead and call and see what's wrong. We'll all take a ten-minute break."

Walking to the pay phone, Jim felt relieved to get away from the five-year planning crap required by corporate finance. As much as he complained about the long hours, late-night emergencies, and lost weekends, he wouldn't want to do anything else but run a manufacturing operation. He loved the noise and activity of a plant running at full speed, and in all honesty, he also loved it when things went wrong and he was needed to step in and solve some crisis. The immediacy and urgency were like an addiction.

He was put through to Eduardo Garcia on the plant floor. Eduardo had to yell in the receiver to be heard over the noise. "We have a problem, Jim, with the pelletizer on the 30-millimeter ZSK. Maintenance doesn't think that they'll have it fixed until the middle of the late shift. And we have to have 2,000 pounds of pellets to Solzar's plant by seven o'clock tomorrow morning. We could shift production to the 70-millimeter, but Chemtrace's material is being run on that machine, which means a complete purging of the extruder, including removal of the screw. The changeover will take about four hours. Should we switch machines or sit tight until maintenance fixes the pelletizer?''

Damn, neither choice was pretty, Jim thought to himself. Eduardo was one of his best workers, so there was no need to question him about the facts. Eduardo's facts were always facts.

"Eduardo, I'll get back to you in ten minutes. Charlie from marketing is here at the meeting, and he'll have to decide what customer he wants to piss off. I knew we should have never tried to run that big of a job on the small ZSK. By the way, tell John when he comes in for the second shift that I'll be coming by the plant after we stop at Pancho's for dinner."

Muttering to himself on the way back to the meeting room, Jim started getting more and more steamed about the time they were wasting going through a ridiculous five-year planning process. He couldn't wait until the meeting was over and he could down some beers and enchiladas before stopping at the plant.

* * * *

The uniformed valet opened the door of the rented Lincoln Continental and, with a friendly but imperial air, said: "Welcome to the Hotel Peachtree. May we park your car, sir?"

It wasn't so much a question as a directive. Of course the answer was going to be yes. After all, the Hotel Peachtree was a first-class hotel, a twenty-five-story tower of glass and marble in one of Atlanta's most prestigious areas. Only a rube would pay $195 for a room and then risk being seen parking his own car.

And Nick Naughton was no rube. A vice-president of information systems for American Products International, Nick was used to the royal treatment. He expected no less.

"Yes, of course," he answered emphatically. "My luggage is in the trunk."

Hotels like the Peachtree always made Nick feel good. Just walking into the lobby erased the stress of the two-hour flight from New York. Richly appointed, the lobby was like gold foil on an expensive Christmas present, providing a clue of the treasures that would be found inside.

Once registered and in his room, Nick Naughton was not disappointed by what he found inside. The immense bedroom had three windows and a corner view. Even the marble bathroom had an eight-foot-high window, allowing someone to sit on the commode and look out over the city below, instantly transforming forgetful guests into exhibitionists if they failed to draw the blind.

A complimentary bottle of wine and two glasses were artfully placed on white linen on the cherry desk, along with a card from the management welcoming him to the Peachtree. Nice touch, he thought.

He was already looking forward to the evening. Glancing at the full-length mirror on the bathroom door, the reflection that bounced back at him was not of a balding, badly overweight fifty-year-old wearing bifocals. No, what he saw was a successful, powerful business executive, a man of action and importance.

The Rolex on his wrist was as big as his ego. It told him that he had thirty minutes to get ready for the cocktail reception and dinner. A few cocktails, an expensive bottle of wine, and a gourmet continental dinner would be his reward for a hard day.

He opened the complimentary bottle of wine, poured a glass, and sat down at the desk to return a few phone messages. One was from the operations director at the Polyresin Division in Bayou. It was quickly set aside because Nick knew what the caller wanted. He wanted to get a specific timetable for the implementation of the inventory control system, which was something that Nick just wasn't prepared to give him. The guy just didn't seem to understand the difficulty in putting in a standard system in eight operating divisions. He was in no mood to hear the complaints from some lightweight in cowboy country. Besides, Nick's boss had just been promoted from chief financial officer to CEO, so the guy's days were numbered anyway if he kept up the complaining.

While making other telephone calls, he used the time to open the conference material left on the desk for him. Packaged in an expensive binder, the material included an agenda for the one-day meeting and a name tag. He read the tag with pride:

Mr. Nick Naughton
Vice-President, Information Systems
American Products International
New Rochelle, New York

A list of the other attendees was also included. He glanced at it quickly to see whom he might try to sit next to at dinner.

Turning the page of the binder, he read the biography on tomorrow's guest speaker, a world-renowned expert on making American industry competitive again. Nick guessed that the speaker got around $25,000 for a four-hour speech, thus explaining why the tuition for the one-day seminar was $2,000. What the hell, Nick thought to himself, I'm worth it.

The Return of Galileo

Surely after the feeding frenzy of cutbacks and downsizing over the last five years in corporate America, people like the vice-president of information systems are an extinct species. Wrong!

The vice-president is a real person. The expensive conference was a real conference, held at an expensive hotel, attended by forty other vice-presidents of information services, all there in the same uniform of dark suits, all there to learn how to make America competitive again, listening to an academic from England, being treated royally by the consulting firm that hosted the conference.*

The money and time being wasted by these captains of industry is not the issue here. The issue is that the conference attendees were so far removed from business reality that they could not even see the irony in the situation. With their heads in the clouds at the top of the ivory tower, the vice-presidents could not see that the real lesson on competitiveness was in the audience, not at the podium with a professor from a nation with serious competitive problems of its own. All they had to do was look in a mirror at themselves, at the ugly fact that *they* were part of the problem.

Information systems can be a potent competitive weapon. Executives heading up information systems deserve to be paid and treated well. That is not in question.

What is in question is the disparity in pay, status, power, and treatment between the staff specialists at corporate head-quarters and the people producing products in the hinterlands. Does it really make sense, and is it really fair, for the vice-president of information systems in our short story to make 55 percent more than the operations director? Why does one stay in a roadside motel and the other in a first-class hotel? Why does one have the time and budget to attend an expensive conference and the other does not?

These questions pale by comparison to the most important question: Why does the vice-president of information systems have more power and influence than the operations director in Bayou, Texas?

Under Max Weber's hierarchical model of organizations, the answer is obvious: The vice-president is higher in the hierarchy, so he has more power and influence. That is the

*As this book was being sent to the publisher, Executive Focus International was advertising its 1993 Executive Forum to be held in Orlando, Florida, where, for a seminar fee of $2,800, the participants could listen to the likes of George F. Will and Lester C. Thurow speak on issues of global competitiveness. A list of early registrations revealed that some of the participants are from companies that have recently downsized, including IBM and Crum & Forster, a subsidiary of Xerox. Apparently, these executives do not see the double standard of spending valuable time and money during hard times to get information that is readily available in books and magazines.

natural order of things. That is the way things have always been.

Before Galileo came along in the sixteenth century, the conventional wisdom at the time held that the sun revolved around the earth. That was the natural order of things, too.

If Galileo were alive today, he would probably question why corporate headquarters are viewed as the center of the corporate universe instead of the plants and offices that make and sell products to the customers. He might question the pecking order of the corporate world.

A mind like Galileo's might envision a different corporate universe. It might see the core of a business as that part of the organization that is closest to the customer and to the product. It might see all the other parts of the organization as revolving around the core, as existing for the primary reason of serving the core. In Galileo's universe, corporate headquarters would revolve around the core, like a moon circling a planet, not the other way around.

Galileo might wonder why, in this age of telecommunications, CEOs still locate their offices in an isolated building, surrounded by corporate staff departments, usually far away from the plants and sales offices that are closest to the customer. He might question why CEOs cannot locate in the field close to the customer and have corporate staff information transmitted to them electronically or through teleconferencing. He might believe that by doing so, CEOs would stay in touch with the marketplace and would send a powerful message to the organization about what and who is truly important.

Galileo might also wonder why business unit managers are so often grilled by corporate staff types during quarterly operations reviews about business results, but the business unit managers are not allowed to grill the corporate staff types in return. Or he might question why factory managers have become so emasculated in America that many cannot even select their own staff in the areas of accounting, purchasing, and human resources, being forced instead to defer to the "experts" at corporate headquarters.

One can imagine Galileo sitting up in heaven having an

argument with Max Weber, the father of hierarchy and bureaucracy, about the natural order of the corporate universe:

Max:	I just can't understand your goofy ideas of planets and moons. Organizations are shaped like pyramids. Period.
Galileo:	And who sits at the top of the pyramid?
Max:	The top people, of course.
Galileo:	Where does the customer sit?
Max:	Uh, er, at the bottom.
Galileo:	And the people who serve the customer?
Max:	Well, I guess next to the bottom.
Galileo:	How you can still believe in that pyramid stuff after watching what's happened to America's competitiveness since that book of yours came out?
Max:	Still a know-it-all, aren't you? No wonder no one liked you on earth.

Returning to the mortal world, let's look briefly at an
example of how Max's pyramid actually operated in an actual
company. Other than changing employee names and titles, the
story accurately portrays what happened when a hierarchical
company kept the core from serving the needs of the customer.

*The company is Continental Illinois National Bank and Trust Company. The
year is 1972, right before America started feeling the pain of global competition. Continental at the time is the eighth-largest bank in America, one of the
most respected financial institutions in Chicago.*

*The trust department alone has 3,000 employees. The trust vault, full of
stocks and bonds held in trust, takes up almost the entire basement of the
impressive neoclassical Continental building on LaSalle Street.*

*The lobby of the commercial bank is three stories high, encased in marble,
and lighted by massive chandeliers. Employees sitting at huge mahogany
desks speak in hushed voices befitting this temple of capitalism.*

*Out of sight to the side are the offices of the trust officers. It is easy to
identify the officers who are higher in the hierarchy. Their offices are
mahogany-paneled and include brass chandeliers and fireplaces.*

A block down Van Buren Street are the so-called back offices of the trust

*department, the bottom of the pyramid. This is where the customer interface
takes place after the trust officer has signed up another wealthy client.*

*Chaos prevails. Stacks of paper sit haphazardly on gray metal desks. The
employees—mostly new and not highly trained—are scurrying about in no
discernible pattern.*

*The walls are institutional green. The floors are dingy, cracked linoleum.
Supervisors sit at metal desks among their people.*

*One of the supervisors is running his fingers through his hair as he
reads the suspense report. Euphemistically titled, the suspense report is really
a screwed-up listing of the stocks, bonds, and dividends that can't be matched
up to any specific account because of poor record-keeping. The total suspense
count for the month is $20 million.*

*It is not the $20 million that is bothering the supervisor. It is the Moran
account that is causing his consternation. Heirs to an oil fortune, the Moran
family has one of the largest trust accounts at the bank. They know the
chairman personally.*

*Unfortunately, the last Moran account statement was short by $1
million, and the family matriarch, Emily, has called the chairman demanding
an answer. The chairman, in turn, called the vice-chairman of the trust
department, who then called the executive vice-president and trust officer for
the account, who then called the senior vice-president of trust operations,
who contacted the vice-president of operations, who marched into the office of
the director of operations, who stormed over to the back office to see the
manager of dividends and stock transfer, who called our poor supervisor to
his desk, demanding an answer in the next two hours.*

*The supervisor knew that there was no answer. Years of neglecting the
back rooms had resulted in record-keeping systems that were beyond repair.
But he would give it his best effort. He would need the help of the trust
officer, though, in searching through the stacks of account records.*

*Calling the officer on the phone, he was put through by the executive
secretary.*

*"Mr. Woodworth, this is Jack O'Reilly at the Van Buren Building. I'm
working on reconciling the Moran account and need your help. Could you
please come over here and help me in reconstructing the investment activity
of the last month?"*

*"Look, Jack, I'd really like to help you, but I'm too busy to go over there.
Why don't you bring the records over here," said the trust officer in an
imperious and commanding voice.*

*"Well, Mr. Woodworth, it's quite a lot of stuff. I'd have to find a porter
with a hand truck."*

*"That's your problem," Mr. Woodworth replied abruptly. "Just get your
butt over here as fast as you can," he said as he hung up the phone.*

Jack O'Reilly, being fairly new to the bank, had committed a major breach of protocol. He had called a senior trust officer directly and had actually asked him to walk over to the back office. He did not know that trust officers NEVER go into the back office.

Continental was later to go belly-up in the biggest bank failure in United States history. Many of the bank officers lost their jobs in the process. Jack O'Reilly quit before the bankruptcy to work at an insurance company across the street.

Circles and Triangles

These three short stories span twenty years and two industries. The first story, set in 1992, spoke about an operations director for a manufacturing company in Bayou, Texas; the second about a vice-president of information systems at the same company; and the third, a supervisor at a major bank in 1972.

The two decades were noted for the massive changes that took place in manufacturing and banking—downsizing, leveraged buyouts, the savings and loan debacle, the loss of manufacturing jobs to overseas competitors, and the elimination of scores of middle management positions. On the positive side, the two decades also saw a refreshing commitment to quality and the empowerment of employees.

But as our three stories suggest, the changes did not necessarily reach the executive suites across the nation. In too many cases, those at the top of organizations remain a world apart from the trials, tribulations, and needs of the people on the firing line at the bottom of organizations. And the gap between the top and bottom has widened, not shrunk, with the formation of self-managing work teams and other forms of leaderless work groups at the bottom. Shaped like circles, these new organization forms do not mesh well with the triangle-shaped pyramids that still exist at the top. Bureaucracy is the inevitable result when the command-and-control hierarchies at the top come into contact with the empowered, nonhierarchical structures at the bottom. Instead of emulating the circles, the pyramid people try to turn the circle people into triangles by making them follow the rules, procedures, policies, and customs of hierarchy.

Hierarchy is the saturated fat of the modern business organization, clogging the corporate information arteries with blockages that slow down decision making. The resulting hardening of the arteries means that the lifeblood of the business, its market and customer information, must be pumped from level to level, from manager to manager, through narrower and narrower information channels. By the time the information has reached the head of the organization, it has been so filtered and delayed that it has lost most of its decision-making value. Then, making matters worse, the decisions based on this incomplete and dated information are relayed back down through the organization, through the same narrow information channels, through the same levels and managers, so that by the time it reaches the arms and legs of the company in sales and operations, it is too late to respond to changed market conditions.

Bureaucracy occurs when business managers lose touch with their customers and with the employees at the bottom of the organization who serve those customers. Hierarchy is what puts distance between the top of an organization and the bottom. It is one of the root causes of bureaucracy. This leads to the next iron law:

Iron Law #6

The greater the hierarchy, the greater the bureaucracy.

Breaking this iron law seems easy. Just flatten the hierarchy and bureaucracy will decrease.

If only things were that easy.

It is a major premise of this book that many of those at the top of large organizations are unwilling to fundamentally change the way they do business and structure their organizations. Call it hubris, call it arrogance, call it ignorance. Whatever it is called, it is keeping the top from seeing—or caring—how their actions permeate down through the pyramid to collect in unsightly puddles in the basement.

If distance between the top and bottom was measured by only physical distance, then delayering the organization would slow the spread of bureaucracy. If distance was measured by only the number of pretentious titles and perks, then correcting these inequities would slow the spread of bureaucracy.

If only things were that easy.

Unfortunately, distance is also a state of mind. It is the ability of people in large bureaucracies to mentally distance themselves from the results of their actions and to somehow rationalize the selfish things that they have to do in order to advance up the pyramid.

It is important to understand bureaucracy at this basic psychological level before turning to other causes and cures of the organizational malady. The next chapter speaks to this point.

4

Dandelion Disease

Sacrificing Fulfillment for Advancement

The advent of complex, hierarchical business organizations at the beginning of the twentieth century changed the nature of work. What had been an economy based on small farms, craftsmen, and small businesses was transformed into an economy of huge industrial concerns based on the specialization of labor.

The concept of the professional manager came into being at the same time. A professional manager does not do work. He manages the work of others. A professional manager does not work with his hands. He works with his head. The output of a professional manager is not tangible products. It is intangible thoughts, ideas, and decisions. A professional manager showers in the morning before going to work. Workers shower at the end of the day before going home.

The Professional Manager

The most important distinction between professional managers and workers is that the former have careers; the latter do not. The professional manager has a career ladder that he can use to climb the hierarchy on the way to more money, power, and prestige. And those with the highest needs for money, power, and prestige invariably make it higher in the hierarchy, since they are more willing to make the sacrifices required to move to the top of the pyramid.

For seventy-five years the system worked well. The career-ist adapted himself to the demands of the organization in the interest of money, power, and prestige. The organization gained a loyal soldier who would accept his mission unques-tionably. Many of the current generation of executives reaped the rewards of this adaptation.

Some also reaped the neurosis that can come along with sacrificing personal fulfillment for advancement. Putting per-sonal values and needs aside as they conformed to the con-formity of the organization, some became emotional cripples who used advancement as a crutch to make up for the loss of a fully balanced personal life.

Douglas LaBier spoke of this loss among careerists in his book, *Modern Madness: The Emotional Fallout of Success*:

> While remaining successful, they experience such symptoms as malaise, alienation, boredom, or dissat-isfaction. They go after and accept as normal and well-adjusted a desire for high success, recognition, and reward. But their career and work experiences have failed to support their personal development beyond the traits and attitudes that are useful for career adaptation. Because of their inner longing for a fuller emotional life, they suffer. They have capacity for greater love of life, concern for others, creative spontaneity, affirmation of truth, and so on. But these have not been stimulated or developed by their career experiences. They remain dormant, as though in suspended animation. When careerists' develop-ment becomes frozen, they become locked into a cycle, in which they are productive as workers, but less productive and alive as people. And in response to recognition of this, which is often semiconscious, they often work and adapt even harder to their ca-reer.[1]

Normalcy vs. Abnormalcy

On the surface, those who rise through the ranks of oppressive hierarchies seem to share some common traits: a high degree of flexibility and adaptability, the ability to always speak calmly and rationally, the ability to control their emotions in public, a high tolerance for tedium and ponderous decision making, and a willingness to hide their true feelings and opinions in order to play the political game and be viewed as a team player. Because these traits have been associated with organizational success for so long, they are viewed as normal and desirable. In fact, some of the more popular and prestigious purveyors of leadership training programs hold these traits up as the model of an effective executive. Independent-minded entrepreneurs like H. Ross Perot, Steve Jobs, Sam Walton, and Jenny Craig would probably fail the programs and be sent to remedial training.

In organizational life, what appears normal and desirable behavior on the surface may not be normal and desirable at a deeper level. Experts in psychoanalysis and psychotherapy know what happens to people psychologically and emotionally when they have to submerge their true selves to conform to the requirements of the hierarchy. They speak of the bizarre and pathological behavior exhibited by their executive patients, many of whom have sadomasochistic tendencies and other sexual problems. Douglas LaBier tells an anecdote about an executive who urinated in his wastebasket before going home each evening.

Normalcy depends on one's perspective. A successful careerist who has made it to the executive ranks of a stifling hierarchy is viewed through the lenses of the organization as normal and well-adjusted. Those who "don't have what it takes" are viewed as abnormal and maladjusted. But who is really normal and who isn't?

Perhaps, just perhaps, the senior executive driving his Lexus to his corporate jet is not well-adjusted. Perhaps, just perhaps, the executive has abnormal power and control needs hiding beneath the symbols of success. Perhaps, just perhaps, the executive is someone to be pitied instead of envied.

It is no accident that the personalities of executives are mirror images of the "personalities" of their organizations. The natural selection process in organizations ensures that those who rise to the top have the values, beliefs, and traits of the enterprise as a whole. If the organization is paternalistic, the top executives will be paternalistic. If the organization is unethical, the top executives will be unethical. If the organization is plodding and bureaucratic, the top executives will be plodding and bureaucratic.

Those with values, beliefs, and traits that are out of the mainstream of a dysfunctional organization can succeed—but at a tremendous cost. They must keep their true selves hidden from view and behave in ways that are uncomfortable and unnatural, thus generating internal stress and a feeling of self-betrayal.

A New Generation

Starting in the mid-1970s, a sea change began to take place in the values of younger managers in organizations. Less accepting of authority and less willing to sacrifice self-fulfillment for advancement and security, the younger managers were quite different from the "organization men" who preceded them. Some were even different enough to be women or minorities. And many were different enough to be divorced or married to working women, which was something virtually unheard of by the top executives who had started their careers in the early 1950s.

Let's bring this rather theoretical discussion to life by looking inside a company with a serious personality disorder. The true story follows one of the newer breed of managers who is trying to keep his self-respect while keeping his place in the hierarchy.

The Greyhound Corporation in 1981 is a large conglomerate on the Fortune 100 list. It has over 100 subsidiaries, 50,000 employees, and $5 billion in *revenues. Some of its businesses are household names: Greyhound Lines, Dial soap, Armour meats. Other businesses are not household names but are leaders in their industries: bus manufacturing, computer leasing, mortgage insurance, food service, money orders.*

The chairman in 1981 is a Harvard Law graduate who had never run a large business before. It was his genius that was responsible for Greyhound's growing from a bus line to a huge conglomerate. He was the one who won a case in the U.S. Supreme Court that permitted regulated businesses to acquire nonregulated businesses, thus paving the way for Greyhound's acquisition binge.

The company has its headquarters tower in Phoenix, Arizona, having moved there from its roots in Chicago. Phoenix was selected after a relocation consultant had recommended it as a good place to do business, even though few of Greyhound's businesses were nearby. Hallway gossip says that the chairman, an avid golfer, wanted to move to Phoenix and had steered the consultants in the right direction. Whatever the truth of the matter, the company had spent a good deal of money moving the senior executives and their families to the Valley of the Sun.

The executive dining room is on the top floor of the Tower. The employee cafeteria is in the basement. One has excellent prepared food and attractive decor. The other has cold sandwiches and a dingy decor. Guess which is which.

One of the vice-presidents, the youngest one, prefers to go out for lunch or grab a sandwich in the employee cafeteria instead of eating in the stuffy executive dining room, with its guarded conversations, tense atmosphere, and rich food. The director of office services keeps sending him memos warning that he will lose his executive dining privileges if he doesn't eat in the dining room once in a while.

On this particular day, the vice-president—we'll call him Bill Marx—is in no mood to eat upstairs. He has just seen one of his friends get demoted in one of the frequent purges that take place in the Tower. When someone mentions the Tower, he automatically thinks of the Tower of London, where the practice of beheading might have been a more humane punishment than what his friend had just experienced.

Right after the demotion, one of the office service bureaucrats—no, storm troopers—had marched into his friend's office to remove his potted plant, which he was no longer entitled to because of his diminished rank in the company. Then came the ultimate humiliation: Workers came with sledge-hammers and saws to tear down the outer wall of his office so that his square footage could be shrunk to match the office standards for his lower status in the hierarchy. Bill could still see his friend sitting at his desk pretending to work as his wall was removed.

Another acquaintance had received an even more severe punishment. The boss, a sycophantic vice-president, had fired Bill's friend by pinning a termination notice on his chair after he had left for lunch.

There were so many terminations at the senior levels of Greyhound that one of the Phoenix newspapers had printed small pictures of the departed executives on the front page. The photos covered the entire page.

The most publicized termination was the abrupt exit of the new president, who lasted less than a year. As the inside story goes, the president had bypassed the chairman and gone directly to the board of directors on a business deal that he viewed as questionable. A fatal mistake.

Next to go was the vice-president of human resources, who had been involved in the search for the president.

Waiting for his number to come up was the vice-president of strategic planning, who was viewed as a protégé of the new president. He did not have to wait long.

Considerable time and energy were spent on the executive floor reading the eyebrows of the chairman for any signs of disfavor. One executive had what he thought was a proven way of knowing when he had displeased the chairman. He would watch for the chairman to begin scratching his elbows, a signal that it was time to change the subject or his position on the matter at hand. The executive was later fired. Bill Marx always wondered if the executive had taken his eyes off the chairman's elbows at the wrong time.

Bill remembers one time he had to meet with the chairman on some issue. The secretary greeted him at the door of his inner sanctum, saying that the chairman would be with him momentarily. A toilet could be heard flushing at that moment in the background. With that, the secretary smiled and said, "The chairman can see you now."

The chairman and his direct reports had bathrooms in their offices. Bill, being at a lower level, had to use a rest room with the common folk, which was just fine with him.

Another time, when Bill was meeting with a different senior executive, the executive stepped into his private bathroom to take care of business. When the executive stepped back into his ostentatious office, Bill could see in horror that he had forgotten to zip up his fly. Within a nanosecond, Bill's now paranoid brain began to process different scenarios. If he mentioned the unzipped fly to the executive, would the executive be embarrassed and unconsciously resent Bill's help? If he didn't mention the unzipped fly, would the executive discover it later and realize that Bill had missed an opportunity to save him from subsequent embarrassment? Bill decided to tell him. If the executive resented Bill's help, he didn't show it—not that it mattered. The executive was later to join the ranks of the Greyhound unemployed.

Being promoted to vice-president at the age of thirty-three had been a flattering experience for Bill. Although he didn't have a private bathroom, he *did have a leather sofa and a corner office looking out on Camelback Mountain. The pay wasn't bad, either.*

But the constant game-playing and jockeying for position was starting to wear on him. The constant fear of losing his job was affecting his family life. He spent half of his time politicking and writing "cover your ass" memos. Thirty more years of this, he thought to himself on a Friday afternoon, and I'll be like the other neurotic executives around here. Hell, I might even begin to like the executive dining room.

Over the weekend Bill made a decision that he had been considering for some time. On Monday morning, the decision had the grapevine jumping: "Did you hear that Bill Marx resigned today?"

"No kidding," was the typical response, followed by the standard question: "Where's he going?"

The answer was a complete surprise: "He's giving up his vice-president title and joining a company that doesn't even have private offices!"

Epilogue: The New Greyhound

The chairman of Greyhound retired the year of Bill Marx's departure and was replaced by the head of Greyhound's food service business, John Teets. Within a couple of years, the new chairman had sold off many of the underperforming Greyhound divisions, including Armour Foods and Greyhound Lines, throwing thousands of employees on the street in the process. Greyhound stock, which had hovered between $12 and $13 for years, doubled in price as a result of the infusion of cash. Since then, the company has changed its name to the Dial Corp and moved into one of the swankiest office towers in the Southwest, complete with an upscale executive dining room and private kitchen adjoining John Teets's office.

It is a testament to the professionalism of his public relations department that Teets is constantly being quoted in the national press, even to the extent of being asked his opinion of presidential candidates by the venerable *New York Times*, as if the ability to sell off dying businesses makes one qualified to speak on national issues. He is known as "Mr. Teets" in the new Dial tower.

Executive dismissals are still commonplace in the renamed Greyhound, and the culture of power, prestige, and perks still permeates the gilded halls. Amazingly, however, many top-notch people remain attracted to the company, and some of the divisions, especially the soap company, are noted for their progressive management practices. But the American-style hierarchy and lack of job security appear to have taken their toll on corporate results, at least as of the writing of this book.

In June 1992, the Phoenix press carried stories of the California Public Employees' Retirement System (CALPERS) expressing dissatisfaction with its investment in Dial and the compensation of Teets. It was reported that CALPERS thought that Dial was a poor performer, ranking in the bottom third of the companies in the Standard & Poor's 500 in terms of total shareholder return. Of particular concern was Teets's 1991 cash compensation of $2.16 million. Earlier, Graef Crystal, the renowned compensation expert, critic of executive pay levels, and author of *In Search of Excess*, had Teets listed as one of the "black hats." According to Crystal, black hats are executives who earn at least 75 percent more than they are worth, based on long-term return to stockholders.

No mention was made in the press reports or by Crystal of any dissatisfaction with the amount of shareholder money spent on the ostentatious Dial headquarters building.

Bill Marx still has no regrets about leaving Greyhound.

Organizational Placebos

Bill Marx was ahead of his time in 1981. Ten years later in the decade of the 1990s, Bill would have a lot of company. More and more executives and managers are dropping out of the corporate rat race, either physically or psychologically. Some have used substance abuse as their escape from the confines of their jobs.

To their credit, companies have responded with substance abuse programs, health and wellness programs, stress reduction programs, and employee assistance programs, which allow employees to seek counseling in confidence with professionals outside the organization. Companies clearly recognize that they have a problem.

To their discredit, these companies are many times treating the symptoms instead of the disease. They are ignoring the dysfunctionality within their organizations that is the root cause of dysfunctional employee behavior.

One does not have to be a psychologist to know that working in a dysfunctional organization takes a toll on self-esteem and self-respect. The constant worrying and kowtowing, and the tenuous holding of position in the hierarchy, create unhealthy levels of stress and anxiety that over time can trigger physical and mental problems.

It would be a mistake to think that Greyhound is an unusual case. Dropouts like Bill Marx can be found throughout corporate America, precisely because Greyhound is not unusual. As a matter of fact, the dysfunctional needs at the top of companies for power, control, and status are so typical that an iron law has been forged:

Iron Law #7

Dysfunctional needs for power, control, and status are satisfied by hierarchy and bureaucracy, but at the expense of personal fulfillment.

Business literature is full of propaganda about the great things that "best-practice" firms are doing in the areas of total quality, employee involvement, and bureaucracy-busting. Some of the articles are so complimentary that they seem to be written as puff-pieces by the corporate public relations staffs.

The truth is that many of the so-called excellent companies are far from being excellent to the people who have to work inside them day-in and day-out. The truth is that there is a sameness in structure and operating style between much of the Fortune 500, primarily because so many key executives move from one firm to another, taking with them their standard ideas of how business should be run and structured. One vendor even makes a decent living collecting organization charts from different companies and selling them to corporate clients.

The next chapter will show how the disease of hierarchy and bureaucracy is spread from big organizations to smaller organizations through disease carriers who are recruited away from the name-brand companies by smaller companies impressed with the big-company credentials of the candidates.

But first, let's end this one with a sign that stock analysts and shareholders might like to start seeing in the lobbies of corporate headquarters:

> Welcome to our unpretentious headquarters.
> We believe in putting our money in plant and equipment,
> in providing our customers with good value for money,
> and giving our shareholders a good return.
> Our executives don't need extravagant offices,
> since we want them to be out-and-about,
> in our plants, with customers,
> or readily approachable by employees.
> We hope you're impressed with our
> philosophies and results,
> and not with our trappings.

Note

1. Douglas LaBier, *Modern Madness: The Emotional Fallout of Success* (Reading, MA: Addison-Wesley, 1986), p. 73.

5

Dandelion Pollen
The Bureaucracy Spreaders

Who are the gatekeepers who control the entry of executives into the upper echelons of corporate America? They are the approximately 2,000 executive search firms in the United States. Specializing in higher-paid positions, the firms have annual billings estimated to be over $1 billion.

The Gatekeepers

The major executive search firms are headquartered in New York, Los Angeles, Chicago, and Dallas. The top three firms alone have combined revenues of approximately $165 million.

The customary fee to find and place an executive is 33 percent of starting compensation, plus expenses. As opposed to contingency firms that get their fee only upon successfully placing a candidate, retained firms get paid by the hiring company in three installments: one-third at the start of the search, one-third a month later, and the final third when the search is completed. If the search is canceled for any reason, the search firm keeps the fees paid to date. A better system for escalating starting salaries could not have been designed on purpose.

The search business is like the car business. The car business depends on changing models every few years and convincing buyers to trade up. The search business relies on the same things.

The search business would not be as large as it is if there was little turnover in the executive ranks or if smaller companies did not want to trade up by hiring people away from larger companies, thus creating openings in the larger companies that people in the smaller companies can be recruited to fill, thus creating openings in the smaller companies. . . .

To find a president of a $200 million company, a search firm might recruit an executive vice-president away from a $500 million company. To find an executive vice-president for a $500 million company, the same firm might recruit a vice-president away from a $200 million company. The iterations are endless and lucrative.

Busy Bees

It is estimated that the average executive will have changed companies five times in his career. Therefore, if that average executive happens to be a bureaucrat, he will spread dandelion pollen from one place to the next, like a bee going from flower to flower. This is the primary reason why dandelions are so widespread in corporate America and why so many companies are organized and operated in the same bureaucratic way. Although there are cultural differences between companies, most large publicly held companies are more similar than dissimilar in terms of bureaucracy and hierarchy. Some companies even seem to go out of their way to make themselves as bureaucratic as the next company.

One company that comes to mind is a mid-sized electronics company. The new CEO, saying all the right buzzwords and taking all the right macho actions, put the company through the standard routine of downsizing immediately after taking over the helm. At the same time, he started a total quality and employee involvement initiative.

Not seeing eye-to-eye with one of his vice-presidents, he initiated a search for a replacement. Naturally, having been recruited himself by Watkins & Watkins (not the real name), the CEO decided to use the same firm to fill the opening. He knew that the firm would find the "right" kind of person, from the "right" kind of Fortune 100 company, with the "right" kind of credentials. Watkins & Watkins could be trusted to use its network of contacts to land someone he could be proud of having on his staff.

And Watkins & Watkins delivered. They found a director-level candidate from a Fortune 50 Company. BSE from Georgia Tech, MBA from Columbia, staff of 100, budget of $10 million.

It never seemed to cross the CEO's mind that he was hiring a bureaucrat—a polished and sophisticated bureaucrat, but a bureaucrat nonetheless. Neither he nor the search consultant ever thought of hiring someone who knew how to operate in a lean environment without a large staff or budget. Instead, they assumed that because the candidate's employer was a big company, he was a good manager who knew the right ways of getting things done. (The same assumption was made about General Motors managers in the 1950s and 1960s.)

The assumption is no longer valid in the 1990s. Take IBM as an example. Yes, Big Blue, because of its huge size and proud history of success, still has immense power in the marketplace and awesome technical prowess. But it is far from being the model of the type of organization that can compete against more nimble and aggressive competitors in a global marketplace. Over the years, it has developed a mid-life paunch and a paternalistic culture of entitlements and security for life.

The possibility exists that candidates from companies like IBM are hierarchical managers. Their expertise is managing big budget programs with a lot of resources and managing other managers who manage other managers. "Lean and mean" is just an abstract term to them.

Returning to the CEO of the electronics company, candidates without big budgets and staffs on their resumes did not get recommended to him by Watkins & Watkins, even though their managerial skills and accomplishments far surpassed the person hired. One rejected candidate in particular had not only accomplished a lot more than the person hired, he had done so in a much tougher environment, in a more competitive market, with one-half the budget and staff. In a rational world, he would have been selected over Mr. Fortune 500, but in a world that measured success in hierarchical terms, he was clearly not as good in the eyes of Watkins & Watkins.

Let's go back in time and follow the rejected candidate on his interview visit to Watkins & Watkins. He'll be given the name of Gary to protect his identity and future job prospects. Having made it through what is known as the "telephone screen," he is there for a face-to-face interview, which he must pass before being recommended for an interview with the client.

Gary has butterflies in his stomach as he steps off the elevator on the 24th floor of a nondescript Park Avenue office tower. This is his first visit to the crème de la crème of search firms. Rehearsing the interview over and over in his mind, he has pictured hours of tough questioning.

The lobby of Watkins & Watkins is what he expected: plush carpet, subdued tones, commanding view of Park Avenue, plenty of glass and wood, expensive furniture. His butterflies are really fluttering now.

The receptionist is stonefaced and unfriendly. The employees coming and going have sallow New York complexions and constipated looks on their faces, as if their underwear is two sizes too small.

Perhaps they are indeed constipated, given how difficult it is to go to the bathroom in New York office towers. The rest rooms are locked at all times, even on the 24th floor, where it is hard to imagine one of the street people taking the elevator to go to the Watkins & Watkins rest room. Maybe the fear is that someone will steal the fixtures.

Want to freshen up before your scheduled interview? You must ask Ms. Stoneface for THE KEY.

While waiting for the interview, Gary glances through the firm's slick and glossy brochure. All of the firm's associates appear to have the same pedigree from Harvard or Yale. All seem to be Wasps from New England. All are dressed in the standard search uniform: dark blue or gray suit, plain-toe, laced shoes; monogrammed shirt; silk ties in muted colors and traditional patterns.

Gary is there for a position paying $150,000, which is considered small potatoes by Watkins & Watkins standards. After all, the firm will earn only a $45,000 fee plus another $15,000 in expenses.

For $60,000, Gary expects the firm to at least know how to interview. Well, Gary is wrong. Interviewing skills are about as easy to find as unlocked rest rooms.

Gary is brought to a small, cluttered office that looks out across a narrow alleyway to a neighboring building. The office is in keeping with the lowly status of the interviewer and the relative unimportance of this particular assignment to Watkins & Watkins.

Talking incessantly, the interviewer seems to have two mouths and one ear. He knows nothing about effective interviewing techniques like active listening, open-ended questions, probing, or paraphrasing. Most of his focus is on chronological history and dimensions like budget and staff, not on accomplishments and behavioral competencies. He does not seem impressed with the fact that Gary's department had half the number of employees as its closest competitor. He was very curious, though, about Gary's reasons for attending a small college in the Midwest.

Basically, all the interviewer knows by the end of the interview is what was on the resume to begin with and what he heard himself say. In a sense, the interviewer has interviewed himself. Two dogs meeting on a street corner for the first time are much better at getting to know each other.

Gary never knew the reasons for not getting passed on to the electronics company for an interview. He could only surmise from the interviewer's line of questioning that it had to do with his alma mater and the size of his department.

The Steroid Business

Search firms are like maternity wards of hospitals. They "give birth" to candidates wanting to enter a new corporate world.

Outplacement firms are like emergency rooms. They take the terminated—er, outplaced—from corporate America, clean up the wounds of downsizing, and send the patients back into the business world to do battle once again. Their fee for doing this dirty work is about one-half that of search firms.

Experts at making the walking wounded presentable again, outplacement counselors are good at helping their clients write resumes that will appeal to search firms and to CEOs like the head of the electronics company. One of their techniques is called "beefing up" the resume. What that means is embellishing the dimensions of past jobs to make the candidate seem as big as possible in hierarchical terms.

Listed below are two versions of a summary statement on a resume for a vice-president of human resources. The "before" statement was the original statement written by the vice-president. The "after" statement was the original statement after it had been beefed up with search firm steroids by the outplacement counselor.

Before

Strong strategic background in all aspects of human resources, plus the ability to develop innovative programs and provide high levels of service with a minimum of staff and resources.

After

Strong strategic background in all aspects of human resources, plus the management of a staff of more than 50 and budgets, assets, and pension funds in excess of $300 million.

Both statements are true, although reference to a staff of 50 in the second statement is a stretch of the truth because it includes people reporting to the vice-president on an indirect or "dotted-line" basis. Guess which statement sells better in a hierarchical and bureaucratic business culture?

The entire search and outplacement process is paradoxical. On the one hand, we have companies downsizing because they are too fat with white-collar jobs. On the other hand, those very outplaced people have trouble getting re-employed unless they look beefy to firms that have just gone through downsizing.

The reason for this paradox? It can be found in the following iron law of bureaucracy:

Iron Law #8

The American business culture is programmed to think hierarchically and bureaucratically.

This law is so important to understanding bureaucracy that the next chapter has been devoted to it. But first, it might be helpful to list some interview questions that can be used for screening out bureaucrats during the recruitment and selection process. The objective of the questions is to get a candidate talking about his views of bureaucracy and hierarchy without asking "giveaway" questions that reveal the views of the interviewer.

- What was the size of your department and budget when you started in your current job? How was your department organized? Please draw an organization chart.
- Please describe what the department looks like now by answering the same questions.
- What procedures, policies, forms, and manuals are you particularly proud of implementing? Why?
- How do you and your company communicate? Memos? Electronic mail? Meetings? Informally? Formally? Which do you consider the most effective?
- What do you consider as being the mission and role of your department? What accomplishments are you particularly proud of? Why?
- In your company, what is the relationship like between line and staff, and between headquarters and the field? What do you think of that relationship?
- Pick a project that you think went very well. Describe in detail how you sold the project, organized it, managed it, and implemented it. Describe the hurdles you had to overcome, any resistance you encountered, the resources you had available, and any help you had to get from above. Please take the next fifteen minutes for your description.
- Whom did you consider as your customers in the company? What would they say about the quality of the services your department provides to them? Do you have service standards? What are they?
- If your internal customers had a choice in using your services, would they? If we call them during reference checking, what will they say to us about that?
- Describe situations where you promoted people. What were the circumstances and reasons?

6

Dandelion Brains
Programmed to Think
Bureaucratically

Battery-powered toys made for young children are based on simple, nonprogrammable electronic circuits. Push a button and the toy responds with a recorded verse, repeating each stanza over and over again until the limits of parental patience are reached.

Unable to change as the child's interests change, the toys eventually end up on the top shelf of a closet when they outlive their usefulness, victims of their programmed predictability.

Hardwired

Corporate America seems to be similarly hardwired. Programmed with certain assumptions and beliefs about how people should be paid and motivated, business leaders continue to respond in predictable, established ways, even when faced with the ultimate consequence of having their businesses closeted away for a lack of competitiveness.

Try suggesting, for example, that conventional compensation practices be replaced with systems that reward teamwork and discourage self-interest and bureaucratic behavior. Go a step further and suggest the abolishment of the traditional merit increase programs found in the vast majority of American corporations. Or, go all the way and suggest that long-term incentive programs and executive bonus systems have little relationship to the health or longevity of the enterprise.

Like pushing a button on a child's toy, the response will be predictable, repetitious, and unchanging: "Are you a socialist? Don't you know that people are motivated by money?"

Just as it is impossible to have a fruitful dialogue with a hardwired toy, it is impossible to discuss the merits of paying people differently with managers who have been programmed all their careers to believe otherwise.

And it will not matter how much evidence is presented to support the different way.

The problem is not one of facts. No, the problem is years of cultural programming, of beliefs that were formed during America's dominance of the world, when unbridled individualism tamed the West and turned the United States into an economic powerhouse, when there were unlimited resources and factories were designed for cheap, unskilled labor. After years of success, people are programmed to believe that the future can be like the past if only the lessons of the past are followed in the future.

This belief is so strong that the lessons of the past keep being taught by prestigious management consulting firms. Push a button and out spews the programmed lesson of the past.

Push the INCENTIVE PAY button and hear a lesson on the value of long-term compensation programs that are based on stock prices instead of market share and quality. The lesson will not mention all of the companies and industries that have lost huge shares to foreign competitors while handsomely rewarding their key executives for stock market cycles.

Push the JOB EVALUATION button and hear a lesson on basing the compensation of a job on the size of the budget and the number of people supervised. The listener will not hear how such systems encourage organizational bloat and empire-building.

Want the standard lesson on how merit pay programs motivate people to work harder? Just push the MERIT PAY button and learn how a differentiation of one or two percentage points will encourage employees to try to outwork each other.

Chances are the lesson will not discuss the alternative of granting team rewards to teams of employees for accomplishing team goals of quality, service, cooperation, and whatever else is important to the success of the operation.

These old lessons worked well in the hierarchical organizations of the past, particularly when America was booming after World War II, when pay and benefits could go nowhere but up, staying in lock-step with profits and market share. Reward systems were totally in sync with the business and organizational realities of the times.

The times have changed, but the reward systems have not, except for some innovations taken by a minority of companies at the lower levels of their organizations. Examples of such innovations include various types of gainsharing programs, primarily for blue-collar employees, which grant workers bonuses for process and quality improvements. Other examples include knowledge-pay programs that pay people more for increasing their knowledge and skill without having to move up the hierarchy.

Want to play detective and snoop out hierarchy and bureaucracy? Then look for the clue called job descriptions.

Job descriptions are a throwback to another age when jobs could stay static for long periods because companies stayed static for long periods. They reflect an era when companies could be multilayered and have a large number of job classifications; when detailed and precise descriptions of jobs were needed to differentiate one job from another.

Today's environment is radically different. Companies of today need to be highly flexible and adaptable, organized into a collection of ever-changing teams staffed with ever-changing members. In such a dynamic organization, team members need to be paid based on competencies that they can pack up in a suitcase of skills and carry around from one team to the next. By the time a job description is written, a team member could have packed his suitcase and moved to his next team assignment.

Despite the requirements of the new environment, the corporate compensation bureaucracy continues with the job description process of ancient history: If a manager in a typical large company wants to create a new job or "upgrade" an existing job, he writes a job description and reviews it with his own human resources representative, who then sends it to the corporate compensation department, where it is either sent back to the human resources representative for changes or evaluated the way it is.

In one company of 5,000 employees, four managers in the corporate human resources department sit down with the compensation manager for six hours a week to read, modify, and evaluate job descriptions sent in by representatives in the divisions. That comes out to thirty hours of management time each week spent on job descriptions, not counting the time spent in the operating units. Does this add value to the enterprise? Do the company's customers really want to pay more for their products because of this activity?

If the truth were known, a professional compensation manager rarely needs a detailed job description to fairly assess the worth of a job—but the bureaucratic process goes on as if it has its own reproductive glands.

As this job description example shows, even companies that want to be nonhierarchical and nonbureaucratic continue to adhere to compensation practices that work against being nonhierarchical and nonbureaucratic. And naturally, as seen in Chapter 1, self-serving consultants have a vested interest in perpetuating these out-of-date and complex practices.

Prophets of the Past

Prophets of the past clearly warned of the dangers of continuing the hierarchical ways of paying and motivating people. They were largely ignored when they made their prophecies, and although most are still alive, they continue to be ignored today.

The best example is W. Edwards Deming, the quality guru. By now, everybody knows the story of how he had to go to Japan to teach quality because his ideas were not accepted in America.

The tragedy is that his ideas are still not accepted in

America. Oh sure, his ideas on quality control techniques have been accepted. But his ideas on how to appraise and reward employees have not been.

Among other important contributions, Deming is known for his "Fourteen Points" on quality, which are really his principles of what makes for a true quality company. One of those points says that individual merit systems based on individual performance measures get in the way of the teamwork needed to produce quality products.

That belief of Deming runs so counter to the American culture of individualism that it is conveniently overlooked in many of the total quality initiatives taking place today. As an example, one executive, making a slide presentation of Deming's points, even went so far as to leave the controversial point out of his presentation, in obvious disagreement with Deming's view of the subject. Galileo was probably up in heaven shaking his head in disgust.

Another brilliant prophet is the noted psychologist Harry Levinson, who wrote the classic *Harvard Business Review* article, "Asinine Attitudes Toward Motivation," in 1973.[1] The year is symbolic. It is around the time that cracks began to appear in America's economic armor. Oh, had we only listed to Harry.

Had we been listening, what we would have heard is this: The prevalent management philosophy is the carrot-and-stick philosophy of motivating employees, which is similar to the carrot-and-stick approach used on jackasses. The underlying assumption of this approach is that employees must be manipulated and controlled from above in order to get them to do what is best for the organization.

To quote from Levinson's 1973 article: "As long as anyone in a leadership role operates with such a reward–punishment attitude toward motivation, he is implicitly assuming that he has (or should have) control over others and that they are in a jackass position with respect to him."

Levinson goes on to talk about the neurotic need for power that drives many executives to want to control others. This need is compounded by what he calls "bureaucratic badlands," which are the traditional bureaucratic, hierarchical organization structures that generate such strong feelings of apathy and futility among the work force. "Most organizations are constructed to fit a hierarchical model," Levinson says in the *Harvard Business Review* article. "People assume that the hierarchical organizational structure is to organizations as the spine is to human beings, that it is both a necessity and a given. As a matter of fact, it is neither a necessity nor a given."

Similar thoughts on motivation were expressed even earlier by Frederick Herzberg in another classic *Harvard Business Review* article, "One More Time: How Do You Motivate Employees?"[2] The article is often misunderstood and trivialized unfairly because it is written humorously. But oh how insightful the article was on human behavior.

Herzberg's thesis was that motivation is not something that is done to people. Motivation does not come down from on high in the form of rewards and punishments. Rather, motivation is internal. It comes from within a person. It is an employee's desire to work hard because his job fulfills his needs for challenge and responsibility.

Sure, money is important, but money is not a motivator in Herzberg's definition of motivation. According to the prophet, money may bring satisfaction or dissatisfaction, but it does not bring motivation. Give someone too little pay and he will be dissatisfied with the unfair treatment. Give him the right amount of pay and he will be satisfied with the fair treatment—satisfied but not necessarily motivated. Give him the right amount of pay *and* a rewarding and fulfilling job, and he will be both satisfied and motivated. It is only the job that brings motivation to the individual. Management, then, can create an environment for motivation by designing meaningful jobs, not by doling out external rewards like a pet owner giving treats to Fido.

And how to do that? By removing controls, increasing accountability, and giving people more authority and information. Sound familiar? Sure. Twenty-five years after Herzberg's article, this is now called "empowerment." It had been called "job enrichment" by Herzberg and then renamed as "participation" in the 1970s, to be renamed once again as "employee involvement" in the 1980s. Whatever the name and whatever the subtle differences behind the names, the idea is the same:

Motivate employees by making work more fulfilling and organizations less stifling.

Predating both Levinson and Herzberg was the noted prophet Abraham Maslow, who wrote in 1954 about the hierarchy of human needs.[3] At the bottom of the hierarchy were the most basic physiological needs (food, for example); at the top were the highest needs for self-realization and accomplishment; and in between were the needs for safety, social recognition, and self-esteem.

Can employees climb to the top of Maslow's hierarchy of human needs by climbing to the top of hierarchical organizations? Perhaps some can. But for the vast majority of employees, it is the massive hierarchy above them that keeps them from achieving true self-realization and accomplishment; it is the hierarchy that stifles motivation and personal growth. In a sense, Maslow's hierarchy is an antihierarchy hierarchy.

Counter Argument

The counter argument to all this is that given enough money, people can be motivated to do anything; therefore, money is indeed a motivator. Okay, without getting into semantics, let's agree that someone's behavior can be influenced by enough money. Let's even go so far as to say that some people can even be influenced to do something unethical or immoral for enough money. Okay, so what?

Is a merit increase one or two percentage points above the average enough money to change behavior? Will people really work harder for those paltry percentages even though their jobs are not fulfilling? If no, can companies really afford the really big money it would take to really motivate people to do things that they are really not excited about doing?

The important issue is not whether someone wins or loses this endless argument. The important issue is whether the argument is even taking place in organizations. Are the key decision makers willing to entertain different ways of rewarding people? Or are they so hardwired and set in their ways that they just want to go on paying people the same way that Tom,

Dick, and Harry down the street are paying their people? Do they want to be part of the herd of conventional compensation practices, or do they want to break out and try new ground?

The questions are key, because if a company wants to be nonbureaucratic and nonhierarchical—if it truly wants employee involvement and total quality—it must think about aligning its reward systems with its new way of operating.

But if it truly wants to remain bureaucratic and hierarchical and is interested only superficially in employee involvement and total quality, then it will stay under the grip of the next iron law:

Iron Law #9

Hierarchical and bureaucratic organizations reward people in hierarchical and bureaucratic ways.

Notes

1. Harry Levinson, "Asinine Attitudes Toward Motivation," *Harvard Business Review* (January–February 1973), p. 70.
2. Frederick Herzberg, "One More Time: How Do You Motivate Employees?" *Harvard Business Review* (January–February 1968), p. 53.
3. A. H. Maslow, *Motivation and Personality* (New York: Harper & Row, 1954).

7

Dandelion Fertilizer
The Perfect Soil for Bureaucracy

The A-word. There is no better treatment than the A-word for keeping business dandelion-free and green with profits. Applied properly, the A-word kills bureaucracy by the roots without harming the flowers of creativity and risk-taking. Applied improperly and carelessly, it can be as harmful to the corporate environment as a harsh weed-killer is to the natural environment.

Some organizations are quite skilled at using the A-word to control the bureaucratic weed. Others seem frightened by the powerful word and keep it from view in a brown paper bag. Still others are quite careless about the word, letting it be used by people without the required skills.

The A-Word

What is the A-word? It is:

ACCOUNTABILITY

There is plenty of evidence to indicate that the proper use of accountability leads to improved organizational performance. Conversely, the disuse of accountability results in poor organizational performance—as proven by the U.S. Congress and other governmental institutions. Unlike the government, profit-making organizations do not have the luxury of operating for long without accountability.

In business organizations, the disuse of accountability is not the issue, for without any accountability businesses would not be in business. Rather, the issue in business organizations is using the A-word improperly by giving it to the wrong people. Misplaced accountability is one of the major sources of bureaucracy, especially if accountability is given to staff people when it rightly belongs to line people. Misplaced accountability provides the perfect fertilizer for the growth of dandelions.

To illustrate the point, the two staff functions of human resources and accounting (controller) will be used as examples. We'll start with human resources.

Human Resources

One of the difficulties in giving accountability to human resources is that the role of human resources is not always clear. Is it a watchdog, a control function, an employee advocate, a technical function, a change agent, an administrative function, or a function with expertise in the behavioral sciences? What is it?

Human resources is not unique among staff departments in being uncertain about its role. It is the nature of staff functions in general to have the same uncertainty, particularly if they are located at company headquarters. But human resources has the most uncertainty. And it, of all staff functions, seems to have the widest range of roles to choose from and the widest range of competencies within its ranks. It is also the one function that, in theory, has expertise in employee motivation, employee rewards, organizational dynamics, and organizational structure—in the factors that have the most impact on hierarchy and bureaucracy.

Without a clear role definition, it is difficult to know what accountability to pin on human resources and what to pin on line management. Nothing better illustrates the point than the fuzziness around who owns the accountability for employee relations.

There are two fundamentally different ways of looking at the accountability for employee relations. The first perspective says that the accountability resides in human resources. This perspective is grounded in the belief that line management cannot be objective and dispassionate enough to treat people fairly and respectfully, primarily because management is preoccupied with the task at hand, with getting the work out the door. As a result, the thinking goes, employees need access to a third-party like human resources (HR) when they cannot get their problems or concerns addressed fairly by their management.

The other perspective says that the primary job of line management is management; that is, the management of people. This is not a responsibility that can, or should, be delegated to someone else. In this perspective, the primary job of HR is to be an advisor and expert resource to line management, not to be a substitute for good management.

The proposition of this book is that the second perspective of assigning accountability for employee relations to line management is the right perspective. The first perspective of assigning it to human resources results in blurred accountability. Admittedly, though, the first perspective is not without merit, since the historical reality is that managers have been evaluated and rewarded over the years for "getting the job done" and not necessarily for their "people skills." Based on that experience, it is certainly understandable why a "people department" was needed to look out for the welfare of people.

That is precisely the point, however. When managers are taken off the hook by shifting their accountability to a staff department, organizations do not get better; they get bigger. Failing to hold management's feet to the fire for the welfare of their people, for example, has led to the establishment of employee relations positions in many human resources departments. The positions are a symbolic reminder, a public admission, that managers are not expected to manage. And, in a sense, the positions keep the issue from being brought to a head. Find a large employee relations staff somewhere and it will be a safe bet that the company does not have good relations within its work force because it does not hold its managers accountable for employee relations.

The issue is an emotional one. A consultant found that out

in an after-dinner speech he was making to a group of mid-level human resources professionals. He suggested that the role of HR is to train managers to be their own employee relations experts, rather than doing it for them. One person quickly waved his hand and, apparently speaking for the group, angrily said: "That won't work. We'll be sued." The consultant did not dare to suggest that companies with large employee relations staffs get sued all the time.

Once accountability is transferred from line management to a staff department, it is seldom returned to its rightful place. Over time, it seems to be natural for the misplaced accountability to reside in staff, where it becomes institutionalized in policies, procedures, and controls. It also becomes institutionalized in jobs—staff jobs that would not be needed if accountability was where it belonged. Bureaucracy is the net result.

The other result of misplacing accountability is that line managers lose valuable opportunities to grow and develop as managers. Without the impetus of accountability behind them, they have little reason to take the time and effort to improve themselves.

This is a moot issue in some companies where self-managing work teams have evolved out of the employee involvement movement. The teams have accountability for their own employee relations, their own safety, their own hiring and firing. These teams demonstrate the efficacy of pushing accountability as far down in the line organization as possible.

There are other examples besides employee relations where accountability has been shifted in the wrong direction from line management to a staff department like human resources. The accountability for training is one of those examples.

Management Training

Much of the management training in America is conducted at the lower levels of organizations. The training is so far removed from organizational reality that the common lament heard from students after taking a management course is: "Great course, but my manager needs to take this. Is he going to attend?"

The answer is no. And the reason given is that the training is not relevant to higher-level managers. Since it is viewed from above as being disconnected from the business, as not helping the bottom line, it is ignored by senior management. As a result, employees get more cynical about company leadership and more dissatisfied with their organizations. In a real sense, companies have established training bureaucracies that sabotage the business instead of adding value to the business.

Until the accountability for the training and development of people is put back where it belongs—back with the managers—training and development will remain a human resources activity instead of an important value-added business function.

Accountability is powerful. It gets things done. Want managers trained to be good managers? Then have the CEO assign that accountability to his executives. Make it a part of their bonuses and a key to getting ahead. Watch how quickly those executives will be meeting in the human resources department with the people who are experts at designing and conducting training programs. Notice how the training all of a sudden becomes relevant to the business. See how the human resources staff is no longer viewed as a bureaucratic necessity. Accountability is a win–win for everyone.

Idealistic? Won't happen? A pipe dream? If so, then dismantle the training bureaucracy and apply the resources to something more productive. Keep in mind, though, that CEOs like Jack Welch at General Electric have put teeth in their training departments by holding managers accountable for managing. It can work!

Performance Appraisals

Another example of misplaced accountability is the conventional performance appraisal process found throughout corporate America.

Well-intentioned, the process is intended to let people know where they stand and, in the spirit of continuous improvement, give them help in improving their abilities and potential. A simple and worthwhile objective, and clearly one of the primary accountabilities of management.

Because managers have not been held accountable for doing this well by their managers, the process has been taken over by human resources, where it has become a bureaucratic exercise largely ignored by senior management. Instead of frequent face-to-face discussions between managers and employees, the process is now a once-a-year administrative requirement that is designed primarily to feed information into the merit increase system. The process is proceduralized, analyzed, and despised. Neither managers nor employees are happy with the lengthy forms and their grammar-school-like rating scales and parental wording. Going through the process reminds employees of their childhood when they had to take their report cards home to Mommy and Daddy. The original intent of the process has been lost in a sea of red tape and impersonality.

Ever notice how many appraisals are written in the third person? For example: "Mr. Cantoni accomplished most of his objectives and is a valued member of my team." Hey, wait a minute. My name is Craig. I'm an adult human being, so talk to me like one—like this: "Craig, I'm pleased that you've accomplished most of your objectives. I consider you a valued member of my team." (Bureaucratic language is one of the sure signs of a bureaucracy. The entire next chapter is devoted to the subject.)

Merit Increases

Dealing with poor performance is another area where human resources has been given the accountability of line management. The conventional merit increase system serves as a perfect way of letting managers off the hook. What does a manager do if he is having a performance problem with an employee? Simple. To send a message to the employee, he just knocks a couple of percentages off the employee's next merit increase. This gives the manager the satisfaction that he is doing something, and it pleases the compensation department, which will see the smaller increase as proof that the system works. Having satisfied the system, the manager is not held accountable for investing time and energy in coaching and counseling the employee, thus leaving the employee with a message but without the help he needs to respond.

To bring this discussion to life, an actual conversation that took place between a group vice-president (GVP) of a large company and the human resources vice-president (HRVP) is paraphrased below. A second conversation is printed after the actual conversation. The second conversation is a fantasy version of the first conversation, showing what might have taken place if the human resources vice-president tried to hold a senior manager accountable for good management.

ACTUAL CONVERSATION

GVP: *I want to talk to you about Joe (a senior vice-president). I've reached the conclusion that he's over his head. He's not hitting his numbers, his better people are leaving, and I get the sense that morale is not good in his unit.*

HRVP: *I agree. How can I help?*

GVP: *Since Joe's strength is sales and marketing, what I want to do is bring in a new vice-president underneath Joe to manage all of the operating functions that presently report to Joe directly. Given his temperament, Joe just can't handle a large span-of-control.*

HRVP: *I see. You want to put another layer of management under Joe?*

GVP: *That's right. And I also want you to find some high-powered executive seminar for Joe to attend. Maybe something like the Harvard Executive Program. You know, something that will appeal to his ego. I'll need your help in packaging this so it's all positive to Joe.*

HRVP: *I don't see any problem with either idea. Can we take a few minutes to talk about the salary and the hiring specifications that you see for the new vice-president?*

FANTASY CONVERSATION

The conversation is the same as above up to the closing statement of the human resources vice-president. Let's pick it up there:

HRVP:	*I don't agree with your ideas because they are sending Joe a mixed message.*
GVP:	*What do you mean?*
HRVP:	*You've recently given Joe a very high-performance evaluation and an above-average bonus. As far as he's concerned, he thinks that he's doing a great job—and his arrogant behavior shows it. Not only that, but adding another layer of management flys in the face of our stated goal of operating as leanly as possible.*
GVP:	[Squirm, squirm, squirm. Fidget, fidget, fidget.]
HRVP:	*I suggest that you sit down with Joe and explain where he's not meeting expectations and where his behavior needs modification. He has to understand that if things don't change for the better, you might have to make a change. I can help you prepare for that conversation if you'd like.*
GVP:	[More squirming and fidgeting.]
HRVP:	*After that, I can be available to help Joe get issues raised from his people about his management style and to put an action plan together for resolving those issues. What do you think?*
GVP:	[Thinks, "I need to replace the human resources vice-president."]

Problems of misplaced accountability like those just illustrated are not unique to human resources. As promised at the beginning of the chapter, the accounting (aka controller or finance) function will also be used to illustrate how accountability is given to staff instead of line, thus causing unnecessary work and red tape.

Accounting

Expense accounts can serve as a perfect example. Virtually anyone who has ever worked in a business organization has a favorite story about them.

No one would deny that some guidelines are necessary on the proper use of expense accounts, particularly in view of Internal Revenue Service rules. But what is necessary inevitably grows into something unnecessary, into something bureaucratic, into something silly and counterproductive.

One company, for example, says that it will not reimburse employees for pay-for-view movies that they watch in their hotel rooms. However, it will pay for an expensive dinner in a nice restaurant, as long as receipts are attached to the expense report. The policy forces employees to take the most expensive option. Instead of maybe eating an $8 pizza in their room while watching a $5 movie, they will spend $10 on a cab ride to eat a $40 meal at an expensive restaurant.

Another company will not permit employees to buy dinner for friends if they stay overnight at the home of those friends on a business trip. So instead of accepting free lodging, employees stay in a hotel at considerably greater expense.

A different company specifies that employees can only call home every other day. The policy is largely ignored because there is no way of keeping accurate records on phone calls, but it still makes employees feel guilty when they have to call home because a child is sick or there is some other family problem.

Perhaps the best example is the president of a California company that was acquired by a larger company headquartered in Connecticut. Managing a global business across various time zones, the president had a car phone in order to be reachable at all times. Right after being acquired and relocating to Connecticut, he asked the office services manager of the new parent company which mobile phone service he should use, only to be told by the bureaucrat: "You are not authorized to have a car phone. You'll need the approval of the CEO for an exception."

The president got his revenge when the parent company was later acquired by ABB Asea Brown Boveri, Ltd., the $26 billion, 215,000-employee Swiss conglomerate, which has only 150 employees at headquarters. One of the first questions the Boveri executives asked the senior management of the new acquisition was, "How can your managers operate in a global business without having car phones?"

The bureaucratic policies in the above examples probably came into being because things got out of hand at some point in the past. Buried somewhere in the corporate archives is undoubtedly some case of a manager who used poor judgment by authorizing something outrageous for himself or an em-

ployee. More than likely, the manager was not held accountable for his lack of management judgment; instead, his accountability, and the accountability of even innocent managers, was
transferred to a staff department. Because the boss did not
look the errant person in the eye and say, "If you do that again
you're out of here," everybody must suffer under the same
inflexible rules and regulations.

Contrast these examples with an organization that is not
afraid to pin the accountability for expense control on the line
operation. In fact, the organization has the courage to pin it on
the bottom of the line organization—on the production workers.

The organization is the Engineered Carbons division of
the billion-dollar J. M. Huber Corporation. It has given members of production teams spending authority to make pur-
chases without maangement approval. This authority was
granted after it was discovered that production output was
being stopped unnecessarily because employees had to waste
time in emergency situations completing the red tape necessary to buy relatively inexpensive parts or tools not carried in
stock.

The examples of this chapter demonstrate how misplaced
accountability creates unnecessary jobs, unproductive activity,
and overly rigid controls. Some of the examples may seem
relatively harmless individually, but, as a reminder, it is the
cumulative effect of hundreds and thousands of such incidents
that result in a weed-bound organization.

Misplaced accountability is a serious matter. It is more
than nitpickers and second-guessers who become burrs in the
saddles of people trying to get real work done. The true harm
of misplaced accountability is that it results in people being
removed from operational reality, which in turn results in
systems, procedures, and measurements that run counter to
business needs.

At General Motors, it resulted in finance experts making
decisions based on traditional financial measurements that
were disconnected from the true needs of the manufacturing
plants, thus misleading GM to mistakenly invest billions in
automation and robotics instead of correctly investing in people

and lean manufacturing methods. At other companies it is the conventional return-on-investment calculations that have misled managers to go against their intuition and make poor investments, mistakenly deferring to the financial experts.[1] The calculations are typically based on measurable savings in direct labor from new machinery instead of the harder-to-measure growth in business that can come from such investments as employee training and improved customer service.

The list of examples could go on and on, but the best way of illustrating the power of the A-word is through the two case studies in Part III, which show how the improper use of accountability harmed two businesses in the marketplace. The cases also show how to get accountability back where it belongs.

It is time for an iron law:

Iron Law #10

Bureacuracy is created by misplaced accountability.

The next chapter ends Part I with the language of the bureaucrat, with bureauspeak.

Note

1. A superb critique of conventional accounting methods can be found in H. Thomas Johnson and Robert S. Kaplan, *Relevance Lost: The Rise and Fall of Management Accounting* (Boston: Harvard Business School Press, 1984).

8

Dandelion Language
The Language of the Bureaucrat

This chapter is dedicated to bureauspeak, to the language of
the bureaucrat, to the officious-sounding gobbledygook designed to obfuscate and mislead. The examples in this chapter
say it all about the muddled mind of the bureaucrat and the
fuzzy thinking that shows itself in the bureaucratic babble of
corporate correspondence.

The examples are real but disguised to protect the guilty.
Translations are provided by the author where necessary and
possible.

The Language of Government

The first examples come from governmental agencies. Although the focus of this book is not on bureaucracy in government, the examples are such masterpieces that they deserve
being put center stage.

The following example is a letter from the Port Authority
of New York and New Jersey, a quasi-governmental agency
responsible for ports, airports, bridges, and other public prop-
erty.

The letter is in response to a simple question from a
community-action group on why federal funds, called Part 150
funds, were not being used by the Port Authority for noise
reduction at its three New York airports. Here is a paragraph
excerpted from the letter:

Part 150 of the FAR was drafted under a Congres-
sional mandate to provide a single standard for the
measurement of aircraft noise and for the definition
of aircraft noise-impact areas using a cumulative application of the selected single event metric. The
single event metric chosen was the "A" weighted
decibel scale and the cumulative standard, the Day–
Night Sound Level (Ldn). The Ldn metric was developed by the United States Environmental Protection
Agency, and it is a widely accepted descriptor of
community noise impact. The threshold of Ldn 65 is
the level at and above which an area is considered to
be noise impacted. . . .*

Translation: "Our interpretation of federal law indicates
that we do not have to use the noise abatement funds."

The next example is from the federal government. The
example is an excerpt from a tax bill of 800 pages released by
the Senate Finance Committee. The example was used on *ABC
News This Week With David Brinkley*, on March 29, 1992.

Sub-paragraph b, in Section 1.G.7 relating to income
included in parents' returns is amended (1) by strik-
ing $1,000 in clause i. and inserting twice the amount
described in paragraph a4.A.ii.I and (2) by amending
sub-clause II or clause ii to read as follows. . . .

Translation: Sorry, this gibberish is impossible to decode.
However, it does explain why the federal government requires
a 15,629-word directive on such arcane matters as the pricing
of cabbages.

The Language of the Corporation

Okay, having set the mood, let's turn to some examples from
corporate life. In reading the following, look for the telltale

---

*This March 9, 1990, letter is from a Port Authority general manager to the
New Jersey Coalition Against Aircraft Noise.

signs of bureauspeak—officious, impersonal language written in a nonconversational style, as if word processors are talking to each other instead of human beings communicating with one another.

EXAMPLE #1

To: R. B. Donohue, Sales Vice-President

Fr: G. S. Franklin, Promotion Support Manager

Re: Your Memo of 5/12/92

> *As per your subject memo, we are researching the history of Price Promotion #18B to establish why the new price sheets were not received by the sales force in advance of the effective date of the promotion. It is unclear from your memo how widespread the problem was or if it was just isolated in certain geographies. Therefore, we will need additional facts on where you think the problem occurred. As you know, we have gotten complaints from sales people in the past that they did not receive the promotions, only to find out later that they had lost them due to their own disorganization.*

> *Please let me know if we can be of further help.*

G. S. Franklin
Promotion Support Manager

cc: T. R. Beardsley, P. C. Cary, R. T. Johnson, S. L. Lewis

Translation: "We screwed up but are not going to admit it."

Here is how a nonbureaucrat in a nonbureaucratic company might have responded:

To: Bob Donohue

Fr: George Franklin

Re: Promotion #18B

Bob, thanks for bringing the problem with this promotion to my attention. It looks like we screwed up at this end in getting the proofs to the printer on schedule. My staff and I feel badly about this and will take steps to provide better service.

EXAMPLE #2

To: All H. R. Employees

Fr: J. McGeevy, H. R. Vice-President

Re: Survey Feedback Questions

Pursuant to my earlier correspondence on the results of the morale improvement survey conducted by the outside research firm, I will be updating you as respects to the status of follow-up items in the interest of furthering communications in the department.

I will hold a department meeting on April 25 in an effort to enhance communications. I will try and answer any business-related questions you may have.

In the interest of saving time, I will answer only presubmitted signed questions, so please submit only those questions you personally feel are appropriate.

J. McGeevy
Vice-President

cc: Executive Committee
All Vice-Presidents

Translation: "I'm going through the motions because I have to, and I really don't want to hear what you have to say." A nonbureaucratic memo might have been:

To: *Fellow Human Resources Employees*

Fr: *Jim McGeevy*

Re: *Your Help in Improving Communications*

You are invited to attend a meeting on April 25 to discuss how I can improve communications in the department.

The morale survey results show that I have not been doing a very good job in keeping you informed. I apologize for that.

Rather than decide in a vacuum what your needs are, I'd like to use the meeting as an opportunity for you to tell me what I should do in the future, what kind of information you'd like to have, and how you want to get the information. I will also answer any immediate questions you may have about the company or the running of the department. To make it easy for you to speak your minds, I've asked Dan to facilitate this first meeting. Please feel free to give him your comments and questions in advance of the meeting if you'd like.

I encourage you to bring up any subject that is important to you. It may take some time for you to feel comfortable doing so, but I hope that the first meeting will set the tone for open communications in the future.

The meeting is scheduled from 8:30 to 11:30, but we'll continue in the afternoon if we need more time.

Thanks for your help.

EXAMPLE #3

To: Headquarters Employees

Fr: T. R. Cook, V. P., Administration

Re: Office Services Requests

It has come to our attention that employees are not using the "Request for Services" form in requesting assistance from the office services staff. Effective immediately, no requests will be answered without being submitted on a signed and approved form. As a reminder of the corporate policy on this subject, the form is to be used for the following requests:

- Connecting new phone equipment or repairing existing equipment.
- Replacing burned out lights and repairing ventilation equipment.
- Moving electrical receptacles and phone jacks.
- Moving office furniture and changing office layouts.
- Hiring temporary employees.

All requests must be signed by the appropriate department manager and the appropriate vice-president. Remember: The assignment of new offices, the purchasing of new furniture, and any major construction plans must also have the approval of the chief executive officer. When signed, the yellow copy is to be kept for your records, and the white and blue copies are to be sent to office services. Requests will be filled on a first-come, first-served basis.

Thank you for your cooperation and your adherence to company policy.

T. R. Cook
Vice-President, Administration

Translation: No translation is necessary. Obviously, T. R. Cook's office services department does not live up to the service in its name. It certainly does not view the headquarters employees as its customers, or it would not ask them to fill out forms to get a lightbulb changed, literally forcing them to sit in the dark until unnecessary approvals are obtained on an unnecessary form. If Mr. Cook ran a retail store, he would probably ask his customers to complete a purchase requisition before buying anything. The amazing thing about Mr. Cook's memo is that no one in the chain of command heard the snickering from the headquarters employees or knew of the stories of people waiting more than a week for a lightbulb—or, worse yet, maybe they heard the complaints but did not care.

Bureaucratic Clues

It might be fun to go through the rest of the stack of useless correspondence, but the above examples are representative enough to demonstrate the bureaucratic mentality behind much business writing. Some of the giveaway clues to that mentality are:

- Memos with initials instead of the first names of the senders. It is T. R. Cook instead of Tom Cook. Oh yes, the bureaucrat also always puts his title after his name, as in T. R. Cook, V. P., Administration.
- Memos that start out with "As per your . . . ," or "In accordance with . . . ," or "Pursuant to. . . ."
- Memos with signature blocks containing the sender's name and title, repeating what is already in the address block.
- Memos with extensive copy lists, particularly those where the copy list is in rank order.
- Memos written with the personal pronouns of "we" and "our" instead of "I," indicating that the writer is unwilling to take personal responsibility.

Verbal Communications

Bureauspeak is not just found in written correspondence. It is used in verbal communications all the time, particularly in large meetings, where no one really speaks his mind when asked for an opinion, choosing instead to use the safe language of tact and diplomacy, similar to what members of the U.S. Congress do when speaking of bitter enemies across the aisle. In Congress, it is "my distinguished colleague" instead of "that flaming liberal who gets his money from union PACs." In business, it is, "Well, let me take some time to think about that interesting suggestion that you've made," instead of, "I disagree with that suggestion for the following reasons."

Electronic Mail

How about electronic mail? Do those systems cut through bureauspeak? Hardly.

In many companies, all salaried employees are on such systems, enabling any employee to type a note (memo) to any another employee, sending the note instantaneously over the phone line by means of a computer terminal. Granted, the systems save secretarial time and paper, and are invaluable in communicating quick, informal notes to people at far-flung locations. However, in the hands of a bureaucrat, the systems are simply another bureaucratic tool, just like a banana republic radio station in the hands of a despotic dictator is another propaganda tool. Technology does not stop bureaucracy.

In one bureaucratic company, the electronic mail system is used so much that all a visitor sees in walking through the executive floor are the backs of the senior executives, who are turned around typing away at the computer consoles behind their desks, resembling chickens pecking away at food on the bottom of their cages. Peck, peck, peck.

The system has become an addiction in that company, giving the executives the illusion that they are in control and doing something meaningful and decisive. It is just so satisfying to be able to send a note 2,000 miles and to get a response thirty seconds later. Like Pavlov's dog, the executives have become so trained to respond quickly to electronic notes that when their computer terminal beeps, indicating that a note has just been received from somewhere, the executives will immediately turn around to glance at the computer screen, even if they are in a meeting with someone. *Beep, beep, beep.*

Never getting enough of the system, the executives have been known to type twenty-page memos instead of picking up the telephone or, worse yet, to send an electronic note to the adjoining office instead of walking over and speaking with the person. *Peck, peck, peck. Beep, beep, beep.*

The chairman of another bureaucratic company has set a different tone. Priding himself as a good writer and student of grammar, his electronic memos have become legendary for their length and frequency. Pity the poor manager who sends the chairman an electronic memo that does not conform to the chairman's idea of good writing. The manager will immediately get a return memo chastising him for his stupidity. The scolding would not be so bad if the chairman would respond to the important content of the memo, but that response usually will be too late by the time it comes—if it comes at all.

This perfectionism has so pervaded the organization that employees are afraid to write anything that the chairman might see. The poor communications manager, whose job it is to keep employees informed of important events in the business, has his writing edited by three levels of management before it goes to the chairman for approval. The manager has become so paranoid and browbeaten over the years, that he spends a good part of his day sitting in his office watching television. As a result, by the time he gets up the courage to write the employee newsletter, the company news is so stale that employees rely on the grapevine to stay up-to-date on what is happening. His performance evaluations and merit increases have been below average because of "his" inability to get the newspaper out on time. Interestingly enough, he had been hired by the company because of his excellent reputation as a reporter for a major newspaper.

Voice Mail

Ah, the scourge of the American customer. The technical invention used to inflict frustration on customers across the land. A device that transfers the expense of having a human switchboard operator from the seller to the buyer. With voice mail, companies selling goods and services no longer need people to answer phone calls. They simply have customers answer their own phone calls by presenting them with an endless menu of options to choose and numerous buttons to push in order to reach an answering machine somewhere in the bowels of the seller's organization. It's kind of an updated version of McDonald's original idea of having customers clean their own tables after eating.

And they call this "Total Quality Management"?

Worse yet, the same thing goes on inside these companies. With voice mail, employees never have to see each other face-to-face, regardless of the complexity of a problem or the number of people required to solve it. Just push a few buttons, send a cryptic message, and let the recipients try to sort out the nuances. Bureaucrats who are skilled voice mail users never have to leave the isolation of their offices for the real world.

And they call this "Total Quality Management"?

Personal Computers

Remember the old days when someone needed a transparency for a presentation that was going to be shown at an in-house meeting on an overhead projector? The presenter would simply write on a blank transparency with a grease pencil or, if he wanted to be fancy, would have a typist quickly type a few bullet points on white bond for copying to a transparency. The entire process would take ten minutes at the most.

Now it can take half a day. First it requires someone who has been trained in Harvard Graphics or some other presentation software. Then it requires the person to have access to a personal computer and a color laser-jet printer, which are commonly tied together through some sort of LAN system.

Invariably, something goes wrong with the LAN system, which requires a call into the MIS department, where the call goes directly into voice mail. Once the LAN is fixed, the presenter is finally given a draft copy of the transparency.

Knowing that the information is now in the computer, he does not hesitate to make minor cosmetic changes to the draft, moving information around simply to make it look nicer. Depending on how bureaucratic the organization is, there can be a number of these time-wasting iterations—all for the sake of an internal presentation and not the external customer.

And they call this "Total Quality Management"?

Eliminating Bureauspeak

The best way to eliminate bureauspeak is to run a business with speed and decisiveness. Bruce Ramsey, the president of the $300 million Avex Electronics company, said it best: "We don't have time around here to write memos." Preferring to meet face-to-face with people, he has furnished his office with a round conference table and one of those white marker boards. Think of that—a fast-moving electronics company, producing six-sigma quality products, that uses a marker board to communicate. How wonderful and nonbureaucratic!

Another way is to altogether eliminate the need for electronic mail and voice mail by eliminating walled offices altogether, as is done by many Japanese companies and a few American companies. Employees sitting next to each other have no need to send messages to each other digitally. They can just lean across their desks and communicate the old-fashioned way—with their analog vocal chords.

Before turning to Part II to see what can be done to root out bureaucracy, let's end this chapter with a final iron law:

Iron Law #11

Bureauspeak is the language of the bureaucrat.

II
Root Removal

9

World Without Dandelions

Why Bureaucracy Does Not Exist on Mars

Want the best lessons on operating bureaucracy-free? The best lessons come from the Martians. After all, there are no dandelions on Mars.

No, not the planet Mars. But the company Mars, the multibillion-dollar (estimated at over $10 billion), world-class company known as Mars, Incorporated, a leader in candy, pet food, rice, and other products. A secretive, privately held company like no other in the United States, Mars is one of only a handful of companies cited by Tom Peters in his best-selling *In Search of Excellence* that is still considered an excellent company.

Because it is so unconventional—and so successful—Mars is living proof that the conventional wisdom about how to run a business may not be wisdom at all. Being hired into Mars from a conventional publicly held company is akin to an earthling trying to survive on the planet Mars, and a new employee can only survive by letting go of most of the beliefs and assumptions learned in a normal business environment. Hardwired people will quickly self-destruct on the red planet.

NOTE: This chapter is based on an article written by the author and published in *The Wall Street Journal* on January 27, 1992.

The Martians

As space travelers approach Mars, the most noticeable features from afar are a lack of assigned parking spaces, private offices, or even partitions between desks. Time clocks are located at the door for everybody to punch in, including senior executives and the billionaire owners. Punch in on time and get a 10 percent punctuality bonus.

Walk into any Mars subsidiary anywhere in the world and see the same office layout of concentric circles, with the president and his (or her) staff at the center and their direct reports at the next circle, their reports at the next, and so on.

Operating in close proximity of each other in the fishbowl at the center, the senior staff is totally visible and accessible. Want to meet with one of them? Just walk over to a vice-president and pull up a chair or, if a chair is unavailable, do what the Martians do—sit on a wastebasket.

When something important happens in the business, watch the president call the senior staff to his desk. At the conclusion of the impromptu meeting, observe the staff going back to their desks to call their departments together for their own impromptu meetings. Like an army of ants going hither and fro, the office is soon a buzz of sound and activity. Communications is fast and open. Memos aren't written and electronic mail systems go unused.

Since subsidiary offices are always connected to a plant, it is an easy walk over to the factory, where the most wondrous sights await the space travelers. Everyone is in white uniforms and bump hats, managers and workers alike. The plant is spotless and shiny, the high-speed lines are marvels of efficiency, and the high-paid, nonunion employees are loyal and proud.

The latest in statistical process/quality control charting may not be seen on the walls, but observe the constant product inspection and tasting—even the tasting of pet food. Watch a whole production run of candy bars be sold to pig farmers because of barely noticeable nicks in the chocolate coating. Better yet, follow a Mars salesperson on a supermarket visit. Watch the employee discard a whole display of product because it is getting too close to the date on the freshness code.

Look for someone with quality in his title and come up empty-handed. Look for people concerned about quality and come up with the entire work force.

This is a lucky day for the space travelers. One of the Mars brothers who owns the business is coming into a subsidiary for another of his frequent visits. He flew in from his office in Virginia, where a headquarters staff of less than 50 runs a far-flung 25,000-employee enterprise. Wearing scuffed cowboy boots and a wrinkled shirt, he has parked a mid-sized rental car in the far end of the employee lot and is walking toward the office.

Unlike most chief executives, he does not head straight for the subsidiary president to review the quarterly results. Instead, he grabs a white smock and bump hat and heads for the factory. His screaming can be heard if he finds unclean or unsafe conditions. And woe to the plant vice-president if less-than-perfect product is coming off the line.

A closer inspection will reveal huge market shares, healthy profits, and such high productivity that the business operates with 30 percent less employees than its closest competitor. With results like these, Mars must have the best merit programs and executive incentive schemes in America. After all, it is the conventional wisdom among earthlings that employees will not work hard unless they can compete for a merit increase one or two percentage points above the average.

The conventional wisdom does not hold true at Mars. Regardless of level, all employees are on a step-increase system, getting the same annual adjustment as everyone else. How about long-term incentive plans for execu-tives? Forget it. That would go against its egalitarian culture.

Employees at Mars have something more motivating than phony merit and incentive systems: a high degree of job security and pay that is pegged at the 90th percentile of the compensation offered by other premier companies. They also share in company profits through a bonus program tied to annual goal achievement.

Moreover, by operating with only six pay levels for white-collar employ-ees and paying all vice-presidents approximately the same salary regardless of the function they head up, Mars finds it easy to frequently transfer people from business unit to business unit and from function to function. Someone heading up human resources today in a billion-dollar business may be heading up manufacturing tomorrow in a $300 million business. As a result, key managers know the business so well that a consistent organizational culture and operating style can be maintained worldwide with few rules and proce-dures.

It is a rare general manager who has not done a tour of duty in manufacturing or marketing in at least two business units. Narrow staff specialists in functions like finance do not make it to general manager.

Financial and business measurements are few but powerful. The most powerful is ROTA (return on total assets), which, in a unique equation, takes into account inventory turns and asset utilization. This measurement, combined with the highly unusual practice of valuing equipment at replace-ment cost instead of book value, gives managers an incentive to replace equipment with the latest technology, thus achieving high levels of efficiency and productivity. The American obsession with cash flows and depreciation does not carry over to the Mars universe.

This is not to suggest that Mars does not have any obsessions. To the contrary, quality is its unrelenting obsession. One example of that obsession is a fear of "incremental degradation," a term used by Mars to describe what can happen by using cheaper ingredients. Rather than replace a high-priced ingredient with a cheaper one, even if taste tests show that the consumer would not notice a difference, Mars will forego the extra profits instead of risking an incremental degradation of the quality of its products. It is more than a cliché at Mars to say that they put their money where their mouth is.

Is there a dark side to Mars? Yes. Just as the planet is a harsh environment, the company can be a stressful place, particularly for higher-level managers who must deal with the impulsiveness and frequent outbursts of the owners. The public outbursts are embarrassing to the recipients, but on the positive side, they become ingrained in the mythology of the company and are a way of the owners reinforcing what is important to them without having to resort to a large corporate staff or thick policy manuals.

Mars is such an alien environment that earthlings cannot survive for long. Accordingly, it is time to return to earth.

Lessons From Mars

What are the lessons to be learned from this voyage to another world? The overriding lesson is that following the conventional wisdom of earth-bound industry may not be wise.

Companies like Mars can force people to face the possibility that their long-held assumptions and beliefs about business may not be valid, that they could be wrong about many things.

Maybe they could be wrong about what a true quality culture looks like, about how business should be measured, about how people should be paid, about the role of senior management, and about the development of management talent.

Maybe, just maybe, many of the prestigious business schools and consulting firms are lost in space with their complicated concepts of the modern organization and their clumsy attempts at mimicking Japan.

One of the most important lessons is how the alien planet keeps dandelions from growing on its surface. Let's compare how the Martian world differs from the planet earth that we saw in Part I.

Chapter 1 spotlighted a corporate safety director who generated bureaucracy by overreacting to the Illinois Wire case. He was adept at putting lightning rods on people's heads to protect against the one-in-a-million chance of getting struck with a bolt out of the blue.

A safe working environment exists on Mars because safety is an important philosophy of the business that has become part of the corporate culture, not because of an alarmist interloper from the corporate staff. The owners take a personal interest in any serious accidents, factories are clean, and machinery is kept in good repair—all without having a corporate safety director at headquarters. Safety is a key responsibility of the plant engineering staff.

There are few lightning bolts on Mars because there are few self-serving bureaucrats at headquarters. Other staff departments besides safety that are missing from headquarters include public relations, employee communications, training, compensation, corporate development, and MIS. The corporate human resources function for this 25,000-employee company consists of one person. Legal has two people; finance, just a handful. MIS is located in a different state from headquarters and is set up as a separate profit-and-loss center.

Mars does not subscribe to the reverse Darwinism discussed in Chapter 2 by letting staff experts evolve directly into general management positions. It adheres to the survival of the fittest by requiring its top managers to have line management experience, preferably in manufacturing, marketing and sales, or some other line operation. In addition, it believes that the best way of developing managers into future leaders is to give them multifunction, multiunit, and multicountry experience. Ivory tower staff experts seldom make it to the top of the pyramid at Mars.

Other chapters in Part I told the stories of an out-of-touch and arrogant MIS vice-president for American Products International, the caste system used by Continental Illinois National Bank, and the trappings of power and status found in the Greyhound Tower.

The Mars story is totally different. As the tour revealed, all employees, including executives, punch a time clock, all park in the same lot, and none have offices or cubicles. Subsidiary offices are connected to factories, ensuring that subsidiary executives and their staffs also stay connected to the core of the business—manufacturing. There are no corporate jets, no perks that differentiate one level from the next, and certainly no executive bathrooms or dining rooms.

And Mars does not allow disease carriers in the door. Granted, it does use executive search firms to fill positions when necessary from the outside, but new hires are expected to leave any bureaucratic baggage with their last employer and to quickly adopt the Mars way of doing things. Needless to say, people with needs for status and perks do not go to work at Mars. Moreover, people who are hardwired into believing that there is only one way to pay and motivate employees do not go to work at Mars; or, if they do, they quickly short-circuit.

Highly decentralized with tough performance goals, the world of Mars is not afraid to use the A-word. The two owners are not at all bashful of looking someone in the eye and saying, "You screwed up." Instead of managing through rules and regulations, the owners manage by instilling a common under-standing of what is important to the success of the business, by selecting senior executives who have that understanding, and then by giving those executives the autonomy to operate in accordance with that understanding. In addition, financial measures and controls are grounded in business reality instead of a standard B-school approach. Valuing assets at replacement cost instead of book value is but one example of that grounding.

All of this is not meant to suggest that Mars is without blemishes. It has plenty of blemishes: It is somewhat hierarchi-cal; it is not a leader in employee involvement or statistical quality/process control; and it has its share of dysfunctional behavior caused by the power and control needs of the people at the top. It has also started to develop a paternalistic culture of entitlements as the organization has begun to mature.

But the Mars culture is also capable of rejuvenating itself, as the case study in Part III will demonstrate. Mars was chosen for the case study precisely because it is so well-run and so nonbureaucratic. The case study shows that dandelions are such persistent and hardy weeds that they can grow even in an environment like Mars. Staying bureaucracy-free requires constant vigilance and quick action, including the application of powerful weed-killers. The remaining chapters in Part II will first describe those weed-killers before demonstrating their application in Part III. The next chapter begins with some thoughts on the best time to begin attacking the bureaucratic weed.

Other Nonbureaucratic Planets

Let's take a quick tour of other planets in the galaxy with nonbureaucratic environments. No, the tour will not visit the planet Wal-Mart and the planet Nucor Steel,[1] two of the most popular tourist attractions. Those dandelion-free planets have become too crowded with visitors, including Wall Street analysts and the popular business press from New York.

Instead, let's take a journey to the center of the American universe. Let's get far away from New York tourists and visit Missouri, where Midwestern values of hard work, friendliness, and unpretentiousness can be seen in the workplace.

The headquarters of Vi-Jon Laboratories, Inc., is about as unpretentious as you can get. Located in a suburb of St. Louis, it is connected to the plant where private-label health and beauty products are manufactured for grocery and drug chains across the nation.

The chief executive officer, John G. Brunner, is the third generation of the Brunner family to lead the 83-year-old business. No ivory tower executive, John Brunner worked as warehouse foreman, forklift driver, maintenance mechanic, production supervisor, personnel manager, operations manager, salesman, vice-president of operations, and executive vice-president before assuming the presidency of the company. Under his leadership, the company has grown at a 20 percent compound annual rate since 1987.

He rises from an old wooden desk handed down from his grandfather to greet a visitor for a tour of the operation. Displayed on the desk is a Vi-Jon "Focus Pledge," which Brunner and every manager has taken. It reads:

FOCUS

I have pledged to be
focused on our *customer . . .*
as a member of the Vi-Jon Team,
coordinating all of my efforts
at the highest level of efficiency
in order to respond to our customers—
faster,
at a *lower* cost,
and with better *quality,*
than the competition.

Brunner lives and breathes the pledge. Speaking with pride about the business, he's off in a flash to the factory right outside his door, with the visitor struggling to keep up with the trim ex-Marine officer.

Employees break into smiles and hellos when they see him. He knows their names and clearly respects and likes them as much as they respect and like him. A family atmosphere pervades the place.

The clean factory is a whir of bottles, filling equipment, labeling machines, and the quick hands of employees placing product in boxes. The operation seems to mirror the energy and enthusiasm of its chief executive. It gives one hope that America may not become a nation of fast-food workers after all.

John Brunner is walking and talking at full steam as he takes the visitor out to the employee parking lot. With typical Midwestern candor, he confesses that management used to park in a different lot than plant employees. Combining the lots confirmed for Brunner the importance of walking in the shoes of his employees.

"See this raised walkway?" Brunner asks the visitor. "It's raised because we didn't realize until the employee lots were combined that the walkway was in a low area that filled with water whenever it rained. It took us getting our dress shoes wet to realize that employees had to slosh through water to get to the door."

Brunner continues with other gems: "When management parked in the front lot and used the front entrance, no one walked through the factory. Now everyone parks out back and walks through the factory two to three times a day. It's amazing what can be learned by coming into contact with the employees."

Staying in touch with employees is just one way that Vi-Jon is able to develop products that meet or exceed the quality of brand-name products of such Fortune 500 giants as Warner-Lambert, Lever, and Procter & Gamble.

Other ways of winning the David–Goliath battles are to operate with more speed, less bureaucracy, and less overhead, enabling Vi-Jon to significantly undercut the slow-moving, name-brand companies in price, passing along the added value to its customers.

Keeping bureaucracy and overhead from growing is an obsession with Brunner, since this is what gives Vi-Jon a competitive advantage in a highly competitive marketplace. He believes that Vi-Jon should only do those things that it does best—those things that are the core of its business. Functions that are tangential to the core of the business are outsourced to specialized vendors who can perform the functions at even a lower cost than Vi-Jon. In some instances, the functions are set up as independent businesses. The printing of labels, for example, used to be done in-house until Vi-Jon management realized that outside printers were much more efficient at printing, because printing was the core of their business.

"When we did printing in-house, it was just a support function, not a priority effort," says Brunner. "Now with our printing activity transformed into a separate, independent printing company at an outside location, they have to compete as an individual business. The marketplace insures they are efficient or else they can't exist."

Brunner explains that as CEO he must constantly resist the natural tendency of people to add overhead costs to the business. "Not too long ago, my maintenance department wanted to buy an expensive lathe," Brunner says to the visitor. "I said no to the idea because we determined that there are a number of premium machine-shop operations—people who do this work every day, with state-of-the-art equipment—competing in the market, who would always do it better than our own part-time efforts. We recognized that teaming up with the experts gave us a competitive advantage."

Brunner also fights the spread of dandelions in the organization. For example, believing that human resources is the responsibility of every manager, he will not establish an isolated human resources function in the company, preferring instead to maintain a personnel administration function that can support every manager by handling needed paperwork without interfering with the business.

Brunner is amazed by the unnecessary bureaucracy and overhead he finds in the name-brand companies, some of which he has visited in the interest of establishing joint ventures. One time he stopped in Phoenix to call on the Dial Corp, only to drive by its towering headquarters office on Central Avenue a couple of times before realizing that the building was Dial's building and not the headquarters of some bank. Brunner's low-cost brain had trouble registering the fact that a fellow manufacturer would be located in such august surroundings. (The reader may remember Dial from Chapter 4.)

John Brunner would have been on much more familiar turf had he just *driven across town to the highly successful and profitable Sigma-Aldrich Corporation, which, like Vi-Jon and Mars, is a dandelion-free planet.*

* * * *

Sigma-Aldrich is located on desolate urban-renewal land near downtown St. Louis, within sight of the St. Louis Arch and other tourist attractions. In 1991, it had sales of $589.4 million and profits of $79.8 million. By contrast, the Dial Corp, with revenues fives times larger, barely outperformed Sigma in bottom-line profits. Dial, however, outperformed Sigma in the race for the nicest headquarters building.

The Sigma-Aldrich headquarters building is just as austere as Mars or Vi-Jon. The president sits on a cushionless chair, in a glass-enclosed office without outside windows, behind a plain table that has no drawers. Most of the employees sit in a large bullpen area.

Like other senior managers, the president answers his own phone, taking calls from customers and employees from around the world, reflecting the company's belief that top management should be more accessible than the janitor.

Although Sigma-Aldrich is in the chemicals business, its senior executives say that it is really in the customer service business. Supplying specialty chemicals to laboratories around the world, it has set the standard for service and quality, priding itself on getting the most obscure chemical to the smallest customer anywhere in the world in twenty-four hours. Its catalog, which contains 51,000 varieties of chemicals, is as well-known in the industry as L. L. Bean's is in the apparel industry.

Coincidentally, Sigma-Aldrich shares Vi-Jon's philosophy about the human resources function, believing that it should be an administrative function only. According to Sigma management, the responsibility for recruiting, testing, training, motivating, and judging employees resides with line management, not with human resources. One executive went so far as to say that "if line management can't do these things, they should be fired."

Like most of the key executives at Sigma, the chairman, Tom Cori, is a chemist by education and trade. His parents shared a Nobel Prize in 1947 for discovering how the body uses glucose. This background enables him to understand the needs of the research chemists who are the company's customers.

Sigma has a very unique management development program. It will hire a senior manager and start him on a forklift, expecting that if the person is any good, he will create his own job and figure out how to make a contribution to the business. Not surprisingly, corporate dandelions stay away from Sigma-Aldrich.

* * * *

Corporate dandelions are also hard to find 250 miles across the state in Kansas City, which is the home of H&R Block, Inc., the highly successful tax preparation, computer services, and temporary agency business. Founded in the 1950s as a private business, and still run by members of the founding Bloch family, H&R Block prides itself on being a frugal company that is the low-cost provider in its industries.

During tax preparation season, the company's ranks swell from 2,000 to 70,000 employees, but the number of headquarters people stays under 200. Highly decentralized, it has only three levels of management between the top of its tax operations division and the tax preparers at the bottom.

Although the company does not formally adhere to a total quality management program, it has always believed in anticipating customer needs. It uses a toll-free 800 number to obtain customer feedback, and it tracks very closely the number of repeat customers who return to H&R Block each year in the highly competitive tax preparation business. That number is an enviable 70 percent.

The president and chief executive officer, Thomas M. Bloch, is as unassuming and unpretentious as John Brunner of Vi-Jon and Tom Cori of Sigma-Aldrich. There is no doubt that he would feel as comfortable in their dandelion-free world as they would in his. And there is little doubt that Bloch, Brunner, and Cori could survive on the planet Mars described at the beginning of this chapter.

Epilogue

It is a shame that so many other American executives have not learned the simple survival techniques of Vi-Jon, Sigma-Aldrich, and H&R Block. It is a shame that New York analysts and business reporters have not journeyed to the center of the American universe to see the real secrets of success. If they did, they would see down-to-earth executives who practice what they preach, who role model the cost-consciousness and customer orientation that they expect in their organizations. They would see hands-on managers who are beating the competition hands-down.

Note

1. A fast-moving and fascinating description of working for Nucor is: Richard Preston, *American Steel* (New York: Prentice-Hall, 1991).

10

Nipped in the Bud
The Best Time for Cutting Bureaucracy

The Seasons

The maturity curve of organizations is a well-known concept. In brief, it says that the lifecycle of businesses is shaped like a parabolic curve, as shown in Figure 10-1.

The start of the curve, Innovation, is the point where an entrepreneur gives birth to a business by developing a product or service innovation. The top of the curve, Maturity, represents the point where the business reaches maturity and stops growing. The end of the curve, Demise, is the point at which the organization declares bankruptcy, is acquired by someone else, or simply closes its doors. The length of the lifecycle varies widely, ranging from a matter of years for a video game company like Atari to almost a century for a retailer like Macy's.

There are a number of distinct and predictable stages between each of these points. Right after innovation comes the stage of chaos. It is a time of high drama, when there is a lack of working capital, meager cash flows, virtually no systems or infrastructure, and not enough people with the right skills doing the right things. The company's toehold in the market is tenuous at best, and the competitors are doing all they can to knock it off its feet.

If the business survives the chaos stage, it usually enters a stage of high growth. Capital is still needed at this stage to

Figure 10-1. The business lifecycle.

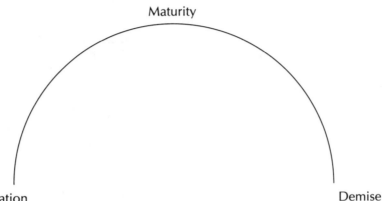

Maturity

Innovation   Demise

fund growth, but financial worries have started to wane as banks and investors begin to recognize the potential of the business. The company has survived the initial onslaught of the competition and now has a clear competitive advantage that gives it a secure toehold in the marketplace. In this high-growth stage, the development of infrastructure lags behind the growth in sales. Efforts are therefore intensified to implement systems for financial reporting, personnel management, payroll, manufacturing, marketing, customer service, inventory control, expense control, auditing, purchasing, credit, collection, and all the other seemingly endless information and processing needs of a growing business. Not much thought is given at this stage to the best way of integrating and harnessing the rapidly developing systems and processes, primarily because profits, bonuses, and promotions seem never-ending during this heady time.

Eventually, the high-growth stage is followed by a slow-growth stage as market demand begins to fall off and the company's unique product and service innovation starts to be copied by others. In terms of bureaucracy, the juncture between high-growth and slow-growth is key. This is the point when companies should stop to reassess their future infrastructure needs relative to their projected growth rates, to ensure that infrastructure does not begin to outpace the slower growth in revenue and turn into bureaucracy. Unfortunately, this rarely happens.

What invariably happens is that the growth in infrastructure continues unabated as the business crosses the juncture between high-growth and slow-growth. Like a 100-car freight train coming through a mountain pass, the growth in infrastructure has a momentum of its own that will carry it all the way through the yellow caution signals of the slow-growth phase, through the red stop signals at the top of the maturity curve, and down the other side, where it enters the stage known as decline. By that point, the business has become so weighed down with unnecessary overhead and non-value-added people that it requires a superhuman effort to stop the runaway train from speeding all the way down the maturity curve and crashing at the end of the line.

The final stage, panic, sets in when the decline has run its course. Those on board the train begin to jettison unnecessary baggage frantically and indiscriminately. People are cut, unprofitable divisions are sold, pay and benefits are scaled back, incentive compensation systems are redesigned, reorganizations become commonplace, investments in plant and equipment are stopped—all of which slow the train's speed but fail to stop it before it is too late. Right before the fatal crash, the engineer and the rest of crew put on their golden parachutes and jump off at the last high trestle, leaving the remaining passengers to survive somehow on their own.

All of the stages of the maturity curve are depicted in Figure 10-2. Much has been written about re-energizing businesses when they become mature so as to avoid sliding down the curve into decline. That is not the subject of this book. The subject is bureaucracy, defined once again as follows:

> **1.** unnecessary activity that adds no value to the enterprise; **2.** a condition of cautiousness, conservatism, and entitlement that develops over time in mature, hierarchical organizations; **3.** a natural phenomenon that occurs when business managers lose touch with their customers and with the employees

Figure 10-2. The maturity curve.

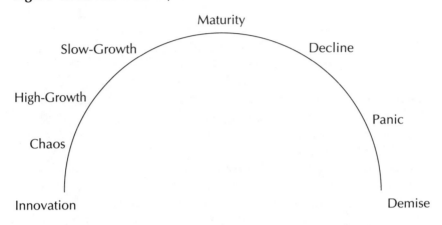

at the bottom of the organization who serve those customers.

A Time for Pruning

Bureaucracy as defined above begins to take hold in organizations at the juncture between the high-growth and slow-growth stages of an organization's lifecycle, at the point where revenues can no longer keep pace with rising overhead. By that point, entrepreneurism has been replaced by unnecessary activity, cautiousness, and the maintenance of the status quo.

All is not lost if the warning signals of slow growth are ignored and the train goes through the juncture without slowing down. There is still time to put the brakes on before reaching the red lights of maturity. But if the train continues on its journey and ignores these stop signals, it is virtually impossible to shed the unnecessary baggage of bureaucracy before the force of gravity takes over and rockets the train down the slope of decline, particularly if a status quo leader is at the controls. The safest and best place to shed bureaucracy, then, is well before the summit of the maturity curve is reached.

History shows that a peculiar aspect of all human organizations, whether businesses, social institutions, governments or nations, is for people to hold on to the status quo until decline has set in and panic or some overwhelming crisis looms over the horizon. Obviously, the worst time for thoughtful change is during periods of decline, when options and resources are scarce and at a premium.

It takes a secure, influential, visionary, and courageous leader to break the grip of the status quo during good times, before the rest of the organization even sees the need for change or the flashing caution signals. Without such leadership, there is nothing to stop the organization from continuing on its suicidal journey through its lifecycle—nothing, that is, but panic or crisis, which may or may not prove successful in turning the organization from its downward course.

The remainder of this book assumes that a strong leader is in control of the organization. It focuses on the actions that such a leader can take to stop bureaucracy prior to the onset of maturity and decline. The book does not address the actions that can be taken during decline and panic. Those actions are in the purview of the professional machete wielders who are adept at wildly slashing jobs and costs, cutting the bone along with the fat.

A Matter of Ethics

Waiting for decline to set in before taking serious action is more than a serious mistake. It is a question of ethics.

Is it ethical, for instance, to lure employees into complacency during good times and then to whack them with the machete of downsizing when the bad times roll around? Is it ethical to throw breadwinners with families and mortgages on the street because the top leadership did not have the courage to put the organization on a diet when the first signs of flab began to appear? Can such leaders look the survivors in the eye and say that they care about their people?

Example after example can be found across the corporate landscape of questionable ethics and/or incompetent leadership. Just look for a mature business that builds a gleaming ego edifice for its corporate headquarters at the same time that its market share has stagnated. It would be considered in bad taste for the CEO to place a bronze statue of himself in the lobby of his headquarters, but it is considered proper for the same CEO to spend millions on a much larger and much more expensive testimonial to himself. Is it just a coincidence that Sears built the 110-story Sears Tower in the mid-1970s and laid off 50,000 employees less than twenty years later?

As this book is being written, the once-invincible IBM, with its acclaimed employment-for-life policy, is laying off thousands of employees. Similarly, the one-time star of Wall Street, American Express, is losing money and looking for a new chief executive to replace Chairman James D. Robinson III, who purportedly conducted a public smear campaign against a former AmEx executive. Nice place! (Interestingly enough, both Robinson and the chairman of IBM, John Akers, had been characterized earlier as "black hats" by the compensation critic, Graef Crystal, who felt that they earned 75% more than they were worth.)

It was not too long ago that IBM and AmEx were held up as shining examples of how to run a business. Executives from these companies and other Fortune 100 corporations were frequently quoted in the business press for doing something wonderful. And organizations like the Conference Board cited the executives as progressive leaders doing progressive things for their employees and their communities.

In the meantime, the real geniuses of American business, the many entrepreneurs running fast-moving entrepreneurial companies, continued to go unnoticed by the popular business press. They were too busy creating jobs and wealth, by carving out niches and surviving on slim margins, to conduct media relations programs or to sit on committees for the Conference Board. Not being high-paid bureaucrats from bloated bureaucracies, they neither had the time nor the money for self-aggrandizement.

Next in Line?

What supposedly invincible company is next in line for a downfall? How about a company that is one of the best-run in

America, Johnson & Johnson? Is it next in line? More than likely not.

J&J, after all, does almost everything right. It is a profitable, decentralized, highly ethical producer of high-quality branded products, dominant in industries with a huge cost-of-entry for would-be competitors. It is not afraid to give its operating units autonomy and let them try new business ventures. It deserves praise for the things it does well and for the superior returns it has given shareholders over the last century.

But in today's fast-changing world, who knows? After all, as recently as a decade ago, a critic of once-invincible IBM would have risked ridicule and scorn.

After attending meetings with J&J executives, one cannot help but wonder if this pharmaceutical and consumer products giant has started to develop a soft underbelly that may be penetrated by hungrier competitors some day in the distant future.

One of the most noticeable things at J&J's headquarters in New Brunswick, New Jersey, is how the executives all look and act alike, like undertakers dressed in well-pressed dark suits and starched shirts, speaking in the same hushed, practiced style, every gesture designed to signal understated professionalism and assurance. The same executive characteristics can be seen in IBM's headquarters in Armonk, New York.

As an example, at one meeting in New Brunswick, a starched-shirt J&J executive was speaking in his best undertaker's voice to an association of human resources vice-presidents about J&J's much-touted family leave policies and on-site daycare centers. Even with all his presentation skills, he seemed surprised when he was asked by a brash member of the audience if similar facilities were made available to plant employees. The executive not so proudly admitted that they were not available, being unable to explain why one group of employees was treated differently than another. He was also unable to explain why the fees for using the daycare center were not any cheaper than the prevailing rate in public facilities in New Jersey, although J&J subsidized its center to some extent.

The executive was apparently unaware of surveys showing that employees give on-site childcare facilities low marks, for the simple reason that they do not want to spend time locked in their cars commuting to work with their misbehaving kids. Most parents prefer to use daycare facilities closer to home.

The point of all this is not that J&J should not get credit for trying to help its employees. Rather, the point is that just because a company is big and rich, its programs and policies may not necessarily be the best, and its executives may not necessarily be the brightest and most creative, no matter how many public speaking seminars they attend or how much discretionary money they have to spend. Chances are that a human resources manager of a $100 million company somewhere in America, with hardly any budget, has single-handedly worked out a childcare program that is much cheaper and much more effective than J&J's. But that human resources manager will not get the public acclaim of his dark-suited counterpart in New Brunswick—nor the big bucks.

One thing is certain about all of this. Business history has shown that today's high-and-mighty can quickly become tomorrow's dinosaurs if they view the world through the myopic lenses of headquarters and if they allow unnecessary activity and expense to build up during the good times. Who knows, maybe lurking around the corner is some sort of government healthcare plan that would drastically affect J&J's pharmaceutical business. Or maybe the Vi-Jons of the world are waiting in a dark alley to steal away J&J's branded consumer business by offering store brands at considerable lower cost. Smart companies have learned to operate as if the worst is happening to them before it actually happens.

One company that seemed to think that the good times of rich government contracts would be around forever is McDonnell Douglas. Like many companies, it has a health club at its headquarters. In July 1992, it announced that it would lay off 4,000 to 5,000 workers and possibly cut production 40 percent in 1994, eliminating another 3,000 jobs in the process.

When the ten-year-old son of John Brunner, the CEO of Vi-Jon, heard about the health club at the family dinner table one evening, he said with surprise, "I thought they made

airplanes there." Maybe McDonnell would see its profits rise
and the job security of its employees increase if they put
Brunner's son on the board of directors. Evidently, the executives at McDonnell cannot see for themselves the awful symbolism of maintaining a health club while laying off employees.

Contrast McDonnell Douglas with the two brothers who
run the Mars world seen in the preceding chapter. Hating
bureaucracy and overhead, and wanting to stay lean and efficient, the owners will resist expanding Mars offices, even
though the business is still in the growth stage. To them, an
expanding office signifies an expanding bureaucracy. By not
adding bricks and mortar to the business, they send a powerful
message to the organization on the importance of keeping
overhead in check.

During the early 1980s, for example, the Mars candy
business in the United States experienced record growth. The
headquarters of that business was literally bursting at the
seams. People were packed together so tightly that it was
common for desks to actually abut against each other and for
supervisors to sit two feet away from their employees, vice-
presidents, and clerks alike. The working environment in the
adjoining factory was actually more pleasant than the office.

Finally conceding that the office infrastructure was lagging
behind the growth in revenue, the owners allowed the construction of a new office building. The building was plain
vanilla and spartan by American standards, and it was intentionally built with just enough square footage to accommodate
the current number of office employees. The dictum of the
owners was clear: "This is all the space you're going to get."
Wow! Talk about an incentive for not adding unnecessary
people! Talk about a symbolic reminder of their antibureau-
cratic philosophy!

In addition to symbolism, Mars also relies on hard measures of productivity and efficiency, and uses these measures
to compare the performance of its business units. Mars is not
the kind of organization that would wait for maturity or decline
to set in before starting to pay attention to headcount and
overhead.

The vast majority of executives and managers interviewed

for this book could not answer these basic questions: "What are your revenues per headquarters employee?" "How does that compare to other companies in your industry?" Most were surprised to discover that there are companies in America with over $50 million in revenue per headquarters employee (total company revenue divided by number of employees at head-quarters). This is of course a very coarse measure that would need to be fine-tuned with other measures, but the point is that some companies do not even track the broader indicators of efficiency and productivity.

11

Roots and All

Eliminating Deep-Rooted Bureaucracy

A typical scene: The executive conference room of a Fortune 100 company. The CEO is holding a confidential meeting with his staff on reorganizing the business. In attendance are the senior vice-presidents of corporate development, manufacturing, sales and marketing, finance, legal, and administration. Absent from the meeting is the vice-president of sales, since he reports to the senior vice-president of sales and marketing; the vice-presidents of human resources and MIS, who both report to the senior vice-president of administration; and the plant vice-presidents, who, along with the vice-president of logistics, report to the senior vice-president of manufacturing.

An outsider from a noted consulting firm had attended the meeting the day before, making a presentation on the alternate ways of organizing— around geography, product, customer, or strategic business unit. The consultant had addressed the related subjects of economies of scale and matrix management. Knowledgeable of trends in the industry, he had also briefed the senior team on how competitors are organized.

The team is almost near an agreement on what they think is the best way of organizing. Interestingly enough, the best way will not affect any of the team members personally. No one at the senior level will lose a significant piece of his organization, other than the senior vice-president of manufacturing, who, nearing retirement, is quite willing to turn the responsibility for logistics over to the senior vice-president of administration.

The biggest losers will be the plant vice-presidents, who, unbeknownst to them, will see their purchasing directors transferred to headquarters under a newly created vice-president of purchasing position that will report to the senior vice-president of administration. The other big loser is the sales department, which will have its training function transferred to the human

112

resources department and its sales promotion department transferred to marketing.

The senior staff believes that these changes will bring about improved lines of communication and economies of scale.

When the new organization is announced, there are basically three reactions from the manufacturing and sales organizations: (1) anger over not being asked to give an opinion on the best way of organizing; (2) disbelief that anyone in their right mind could have come up with anything so stupid; and (3) resentment that they were being treated like second-class citizens again by the senior muckywuks.

The reaction from headquarters employees is just the opposite. The feeling is universal that it was about time that the senior staff got the organization straightened out.

A Political Problem

The above scene actually happened. It is typical because it represents the top-down approach to reorganizing companies, an approach that is totally removed from the needs of the customers, an approach that ignores the people at the bottom of the organization who must try to meet those customer needs day-in and day-out. It is the Galileo problem revisited; namely, the tendency of those at the top of a hierarchy to view head-quarters as the center of the universe, as the core of the business. It is considered heresy by those in power to suggest that the reverse is true.

Heresy is not the real issue here. The real issue is one of power and status, of people in positions of power afraid of losing their status if the organization is redesigned from the ground-floor-up and the outside-in. Because it touches the raw nerve of power and status, the issue becomes a political issue, an issue of competing interests and winners and losers.

What is needed is a change process that circumvents the political system in the company by bringing objective information from the bottom directly to the chief executive officer or business unit head, bypassing any biased, self-serving, or out-of-touch management levels in between that may act like information filters.

Once again, only a secure, confident and courageous top

manager can overcome the political problem and take an objective look at the needs of the core. To do otherwise only perpetuates the bureaucracy and the status quo.

As a reminder, this book is based on the belief that bureaucracy will grow back unless it is pulled out by the roots. As shown in Part I, some of the longest and most intractable roots of bureaucracy are those of misplaced accountability between line and staff, undue influence and power at headquarters, and a hierarchical organization structure.

These roots are the primary reason why many of the efforts at total quality, re-engineering and employee involvement have proven to have limited or temporary success. Only cutting off the dandelion flower on the surface, these efforts have not gotten to the roots that are really keeping substantial, organizationwide change from happening. Sooner or later, the roots will grow back into new dandelion flowers, only to trigger another cycle of surface dandelion cutting in the form of new programs, new cost cutting, and new downsizing.

Root Removal Steps

The following are the steps that can be taken to remove the deeper and more intractable roots of bureaucracy. These steps ideally should be taken first and then followed up with weed-control treatments described in subsequent chapters. The steps are based on the assumption that a strong leader is in charge of the organizational unit and wants to eliminate bureaucracy, by the roots, by reorganizing the business around the needs of the customer and the employees at the bottom of the organization. The steps are applicable to an entire company, a division of a company, or some other organizational unit like a manufacturing facility.

Step 1: Appoint an Independent Project Leader

The person appointed to head up a root removal project has to be someone trusted by the CEO (or other organizational head sponsoring the project) and viewed by the other executives as impartial, apolitical, and not seeking a higher position. Sometimes the best candidates are line executives nearing retirement age, those in a training and development function, or those who have experience in total quality or re-engineering.

An alternative is to hire an outside consultant, although this option is suggested with serious reservations, the reason being that there are so many self-serving consultants doing so many simplistic, superficial, and harmful things to organizations.

Want a total quality culture in a matter of weeks? An unprincipled consultant can be found to put all employees through a canned, four-day training program, teaching them how to measure anything that moves or breathes. Want improved productivity? A dishonest consultant can be found to suggest that a new incentive pay plan is the answer. (As an interesting side note, Tomohiro Takamoto of the Nomura Research Institute, Ltd., in a study conducted for the author, estimated that management consulting in the United States, in 1990, was a $13 billion industry, versus $1.5 billion in Japan.)

The type of consultant needed to guide an organization through root removal is known in the trade as an organization effectiveness/development consultant. This type of consultant has expertise in applying the behavioral sciences to organizations and in guiding businesses through major, companywide change efforts. The Organization Development Network or the National Training Labs are good sources of referrals for organization effectiveness consultants.

An independent project leader or consultant is needed for a multiplicity of reasons, but the primary one is to help the CEO walk through the political mine field without harming himself or the organization. Inevitably, a root removal project will be threatening and embarrassing to any close-minded executives who have never before received unfiltered feedback from internal and external customers on the performance of their departments. Some managers have such unhealthy and unrealistic views of themselves, and such power and control needs, that their egos cannot tolerate the truth, no matter how constructively and sensitively it is presented.

On the bright side, the majority of managers want to do a

good job and will use the project as an opportunity to learn and develop. The project will also give the CEO the opportunity to see his people in a new light, enabling him to determine which ones are willing to work for the good of the organization and which ones are driven by purely selfish motives.

Step 2: Develop Broad-Based Support and a Common Understanding

The overall purpose of this step is for the CEO to get as much support as he can for the project among his senior staff and to communicate the objectives and timetable for the root-removal project to the entire organization. It includes a number of substeps.

1. With the help of the project leader, the CEO develops his vision of the future organization—what it may look like and how it may operate.
2. In addition, he develops a preliminary project plan and timetable.
3. He introduces his preliminary thoughts to his staff at a fairly short meeting.
4. After the meeting, the project leader schedules individual private meetings with each staff member to get each person's concerns, reactions, and suggestions.
5. Using this input, the CEO holds a two-day offsite meeting with his staff to resolve any issues and to develop a firm project plan.
6. After the offsite meeting, the CEO lets the rest of the organization know about the project, using normal communication channels. If true and appropriate, the CEO assures the organization that the project is not a downsizing effort in disguise.

Step 3: Form Project Team

Selection of project team members to work with the project leader full-time for the duration of the project is key to the success of the root removal. Team members must come from all functions in the company and must be viewed as experienced, bright, honest, nonpolitical, and hard-working. Ideally, each of the CEO's vice-presidents will select a trusted management-level person for the team, but, more important, team members will also be selected from each of the line operations outside of corporate headquarters. In a manufacturing business, this might include a representative(s) from each plant and each sales region. In a service business, this would include whomever is considered as the core of the business. It is critical to the success of the project for the members from the line operation to be the majority on the team, to ensure that the perspectives of those closest to the customer prevail.

Step 4: Train Project Team

In this step, the project leader trains the team members in how to diagnose organizational ills, using certain techniques based on a certain principles.

First the techniques. The project team will be taught how to:

• Conduct structured interviews with outside customers to determine how well customer requirements, needs, expectations, and standards are being met.

• Conduct structured interviews with internal "customers," starting at the bottom of the organization, to determine how well the requirements, needs, expectations, and standards of the people at the bottom are being met by their "suppliers" at the next higher level of the organization. Used here, the word "bottom" really means bottom. In a manufacturing business, bottom is the production worker on the production line.

• Keep track of variances using variance analysis charts, which show where services or products being provided upstream in the organization are not meeting the expectations, needs, and standards of downstream customers.

• Follow information flows and business processes from the customers at the bottom of the organization to the top of the organization. An example of an information flow might be a computer-generated list of accounts used by a salesperson. If that list is not accurate or timely, the information flow would be tracked back through the organization to the source of the problem. An example of a business process might be the way that shipments get to the customer. If those shipments are not timely, the business process of filling customer orders would be tracked from the loading dock, through shipping, through production, into customer service, into billing, through transportation, through sales, and through any other function that may have an impact on timely deliveries.

• Chart the key information flows and business processes in order to begin developing some preliminary ideas on a more effective organization structure, using certain principles.

And here are the principles that guide the techniques:

• *Whole Jobs*. Whole jobs are jobs that include responsibilities for doing, controlling, and planning. Whole jobs are the basic building block of effective organizations; they provide the foundation for building an organization with few layers of management and with a framework for employee involvement and total quality.

The concept is to give controlling and planning responsibilities to every person, instead of restricting lower-level people to just "doing" and reserving controlling and planning to people higher in the organization. It is important for the project team members to be able to think of nonhierarchical and nontraditional ways of designing jobs. That way, the organization will have a minimum of rules and regulations, and few checkers checking checkers.

• *Accountability*. This principle is simple. It means that jobs will not be created because other people are not doing their jobs. It assumes that people are competent, or if they are not competent, they will be given remedial training or dealt with appropriately. Under this principle, the existence of employee relations positions at corporate headquarters would be questioned by the project team, as well as any other jobs that belong in line operations instead of staff, and vice versa.

• *Decentralization.* Related to the first two principles, this means pushing responsibility as far down in the organization as possible. Centralized functions should be restricted to those activities that have to be done at the corporate level (e.g., financial reporting to the government), to those where there is a clear economic advantage that far outweighs any loss of freedom at the operating level (e.g., some MIS functions), and to those that are strategic in nature and cross business unit boundaries (e.g., possibly corporate development). The underlying guideline, however, is that what gets centralized and decentralized should be based on an objective analysis and not on the opinions of politicians in pursuit of power and status.*

• *Effective Units.* An effective unit is a division, plant, or other organizational component that is neither too large nor too small. It is large enough to be self-sufficient and small enough to operate nonbureaucratically with speed and decisiveness. Generally, the ideal size of an organization is 500 employees or less.

• *Teams.* Teams are an effective way of organizing horizontally to handle business processes that cross through the vertical walls of the functional organization. As an example, a logistics team might consist of someone from the transportation department, someone from receiving, someone from customer orders, someone from the finished-good warehouse, someone from shipping, and so on. The team members still report to their respective functional departments for administrative and training purposes, but they work together under a team leader on day-to-day operational issues.

Step 5: Begin Diagnosing the Organization

After the project team members are trained, they break into smaller teams and begin to use the aforementioned techniques

---

*Amazingly, as this chapter was being written, IBM announced that it was forming a centralized recruiting and staffing function at headquarters that would operate as a profit-and-loss center by providing services to the operating units. Here is a company that has laid off over 100,000 people because it had lost touch with the marketplace, but it still believes in centralized functions because of the cost "savings" of doing things centrally, apparently not understanding the immeasurable benefit of giving operating units the freedom to select their own people.

and principles to study the organization. The project leader helps to keep the team members on track and to coordinate the work of the various subteams.

Step 6: Calibrate Initial Findings

As the team begins to uncover significant problems, it is important that the team members, with the help of the team leader, present those initial findings to the senior staff and the CEO. Invariably, the senior staff will have comments, criticisms, and suggestions; sometimes they will be able to give a perspective on an issue that the team members could not see from their level. If by chance the team is met with extreme defensiveness or denial, the project leader may suggest that the senior staff participate in the more sensitive parts of the diagnosis along with the team, particularly on the visits to outside customers. The calibration step should be repeated many times during the duration of the project.

Step 7: Develop Straw Man Organization Structure

This is the most difficult and sensitive step of the project. It is the step in which the team members realize that what they are doing will affect a large number of their associates in the organization. Tensions run high as team members go through the exhausting process of analyzing the data acquired in the preceding steps, realizing at some point that not all of their decisions can be made analytically; some will have to be made through the intuition gained from months of seeing how the organization really works.

Step 8: Present Straw Man Organization

The straw man organization is first presented to the CEO, who must then decide how much say in changing the proposal he will give his direct reports, some of whom might be affected personally by the proposed structure. At some point, though, the proposal or parts of it must go before the senior staff for review and modification.

Step 9: Develop Final Organization and Implementation Plan

Based on the suggestions of the CEO and his staff, the project team puts the finishing touches on the organization and develops a detailed implementation plan. The plan will address such issues as:

1. Communications to employees and affected people.
2. Suggestions on how to place excess people in the organization. (There will undoubtedly be a number of jobs eliminated as a result of the project. Senior management will have to decide whether to lay off the incumbents or transfer them to revenue-generating positions in the new organization.)
3. Training of people for their new roles.
4. How to get the above done in a timely and orderly fashion.

Step 10: Implement Plan

At this point, the project team is disbanded and the members return to their respective departments. However, the team will be brought together periodically by the senior staff to help out on problems or questions arising from the implementation.

As can be seen from the above steps, root pulling is not an easy task. It is much easier for the senior staff to reorganize quickly, as in the vignette at the beginning of this chapter. Like a suburban homeowner cutting his grass, it is much quicker to just lop off the heads of the dandelions. It is considerably harder and more time-consuming to stop the lawn mower and dig up the weeds by the roots. There is no doubt, though, which method of controlling the spread of dandelions is more effective. Just how effective will be shown in the case study in Part III.

12

Gardening Secrets
Other Methods of Eliminating Bureaucracy

Chapter 11 described a method of redesigning organizations from the bottom-up and outside-in; that is, from the requirements of the external customers and the employees at the bottom of the organization who serve those customers. The method is particularly useful against the more deep-rooted, entrenched bureaucracy found in large, mature businesses. It is one of the best methods of breaking the iron laws of bureaucracy.

Additional methods of breaking the iron laws are described in this chapter. The additional methods are less potent than the one in the previous chapter and can be used effectively only on dandelions that are not as deep-rooted or resistant. Before discussing the methods, it might be helpful to first list all the iron laws:

The Iron Laws of Bureaucracy

Iron Law #1

Staff employees with unfulfilled needs for status, recognition, and power will create bureaucracy to satisfy those needs.

Iron Law #2

Self-serving outside consultants will create bureaucracy by selling unneeded services.

Iron Law #3

Bureaucracy takes over slowly, one small seed at a time, until the organization is so weed-bound that it loses sight of the competition.

Iron Law #4

Bureaucratic organizations are the natural offspring of bureaucratic managers.

Iron Law #5

Bureaucratic managers are the natural offspring of bureaucratic organizations.

Iron Law #6

The greater the hierarchy, the greater the bureaucracy.

Iron Law #7

Dysfunctional needs for power, control, and status are satisfied by hierarchy and bureaucracy, but at the expense of personal fulfillment.

Iron Law #8

The American business culture is programmed to think hierarchically and bureaucratically.

Iron Law #9

Hierarchical and bureaucratic organizations reward people in hierarchical and bureaucratic ways.

Iron Law #10

Bureaucracy is created by misplaced accountability.

Iron Law #11

Bureauspeak is the langauge of the bureaucrat.

Additional Lawbreakers

1. *Rotating managers between line and staff positions, thus bringing a sense of operational reality to corporate headquarters.* Successful companies like Mars will not promote managers to general manager unless they have had their "ticket punched" in a variety of line and staff jobs.

2. *Implementing compensation and job evaluation systems that facilitate this rotation.* Conventional compensation systems sometimes put a higher value on corporate staff positions than on line operation positions (probably because corporate staff controls the systems). As long as the reward systems penalize staff people from taking developmental assignments in operations, few will be willing to accept such transfers.

3. *Requiring executives to work in jobs at the bottom of the organization at least a couple of days a month.* To get an unfiltered dose of reality, and to set an important example, executives should work periodically in production, customer service, sales, or other functions that interface directly with the customer.

4. *Requiring executives to hold private meetings with employees and groups of employees, selected at random from all functions and levels of the company.* The purpose of the meetings would be for the executives to get unfiltered feedback from employees on the problems they face in producing quality products and services.

5. *Implementing job evaluation systems that discourage bureaucracy and hierarchy.* Many evaluation systems assign points to jobs based on such dimensions as the number of people supervised, the pay grade of the direct reports, and the size of the budget and payroll. Naturally, people react to these systems by increasing their dimensions. A much better system is to base the worth of a job on the additional value it brings to the organization. That way, someone in an entrepreneurial role with few traditional job dimensions could earn more than someone whose job it is to maintain a current book of business.

6. *Replacing traditional performance appraisal programs with performance feedback systems that give managers feedback not only*

from above, but also from peers, subordinates, and "downstream"
internal customers. The feedback would be in the areas of teamwork, leadership, ethics, participation, and commitment to
quality. Once gathered and summarized, the feedback could
be used for developmental planning and as a basis for bonus
payments. (A favorite fantasy is that boards of directors will
start requiring CEOs to gather such feedback on themselves
and report it, along with financial information, to the directors.)

7. *Replacing traditional merit pay programs with team-based*
rewards and knowledge-pay programs. Team-based rewards are
essential for organizations using teams as their basic building
block. Also, knowledge-pay programs are a good way of rewarding employees for increasing their knowledge and skill
without having to move up the hierarchy to a job with a bigger
title.

8. *Establishing allocation systems whereby the line operations*
have the authority to negotiate the budgets of staff departments. This
is only advisable if the line truly has power and influence in
the organization. If not, the allocation systems will become a
politicized, bureaucratic waste of time.

9. *Selecting people for leadership positions who do not have*
dysfunctional needs for power, status, and control. There are a
variety of proven assessment techniques and psychological
instruments for weeding out egocentric, power hungry individ-
uals—and keeping them out of the executive suite.

10. *Assigning the accountability for regulatory compliance to*
operations instead of to staff experts at headquarters. In the safety
director vignette of Chapter 1, for example, the safety function
would have been better served by having it reside in manufacturing or engineering at the divisional level instead of at headquarters, where the incumbent was tempted to expand his
authority well beyond the needs of the plants. A word of
caution: It is difficult to overcome the typical bean counter
argument of the economies of scale that accrue by doing things
centrally. The best way of overcoming this argument is for
headquarter executives to experience firsthand how centralized
staff functions take away the freedom and flexibility needed at

the bottom of the organization to respond quickly to changed market conditions and operational realities.

11. *Outsourcing staff advisory functions to independent contractors, specifying the limits of their expenditures, and establishing clear performance standards.* Using the safety function as an example again, an external safety advisor operating under contract will not be tempted to expand his authority and interfere with the prerogatives of line management in order to climb the hierarchy in pursuit of more status and pay. Just as important, he will not require direct supervision, merit increases, performance appraisals, an office, a desk, supplies, floor space, lights, and all the other expenses that come with full-time employees.

12. *Assigning certain audit and control functions to line managers on a rotational basis.* As an example, plant managers can take turns auditing each other on adherence to safety policies and procedures.

13. *Having a team of line managers review the necessity of all existing policies and controls.* The team would have the authority to eliminate two types of policies and controls: (a) those that exist only because a small fraction of employees do not have the good judgment or training to operate without corporate directives; or (b) those that keep managers from being held accountable for being good managers.

14. *Redesigning offices for easy face-to-face communications without having to rely on electronic mail or voice mail.* For office productivity to increase to the level attained in manufacturing operations, offices will need to start looking and operating more like factories, with people in eyesight of each other who jump on problems immediately, get them solved, and move on to the next problem—all without the aid of electronic communications, fancy reports, and multicolored graphs.

15. *Eliminating all symbols of excess, double standards, and we–they mentality.* The symbols of hierarchy have to be removed and placed in the museum of outdated management practices. Private bathrooms, executive dining rooms, reserved parking spaces, private secretaries, executive suites—all should be placed on exhibit in the Smithsonian.

13

Lawn Treatments
Keeping Bureaucracy From Growing Back

So far, Part II of this book has covered the following: Chapter 9 described the dandelion-free world of Mars and other companies; Chapter 10 discussed the best time in the growing season for removing corporate dandelions; Chapter 11 outlined how to remove the most stubborn bureaucratic weeds, roots and all, from the corporate landscape; and Chapter 12 listed ways of uprooting less stubborn dandelions.

This chapter describes proven treatments that should be applied, once the hard work of removing dandelions is done, to develop a healthy organizational turf, green with profits and dandelion-resistant.

The treatments are as follows:

- Team-building
- Employee involvement
- Total quality management
- Team organizations
- Business process re-engineering

Because these treatments exist in varying degrees in corporate America, the reader may be familiar with some or all of them. The purpose of this discussion, then, is to provide a brief refresher on what the treatments are intended to accomplish and what precautions should be taken before using them, just as the label of instructions and warnings on a bottle of weed-killer should be read by the homeowner before spraying his bluegrass. It is important to understand how the various treatments should be used in conjunction with one another as part of a planned approach to organization effectiveness.

The average homeowner realizes that it would be counter-productive and possibly dangerous to start spraying his lawn indiscriminately with a little of this and a little of that, without any set dosages or environmental protection. It is sad to say, but all too many corporate chieftains have not learned the lesson of the average homeowner. They have bought a little of this from one consultant and a little of that from another consultant, without having an overall treatment plan or under-standing the interactions between the different approaches to building an effective organization. Not surprisingly, the results of this experimental mixing have been disappointing or, in the worst cases, actually harmful to the corporate environment.

With that thought in mind, let's read the instructions and warning labels on the treatments that should be applied to the corporate landscape to keep it dandelion-free.

Team-Building

Team-building is a process that a natural work group (usually a boss and his subordinates) goes through to address issues of trust, communications, cooperation, and leadership that get in the way of effective planning, decision making, and problem solving within the team.

Usually done with the assistance of an outside facilitator trained in the behavioral sciences and small group dynamics, team-building surfaces any serious issues among the team members that have become submerged over time. Typically, team-building is needed periodically even in the best teams, for it is natural for team members to get so caught up in the press of business that they fail to check if the team is truly functioning as a team, with the team members rowing in the same direction, under focused leadership, toward common goals. Teams are like spouses who grow apart because they forget to take care of the relationship as they get caught up in their careers and raising their family.

It is essential for team-building to begin at the top of the organization with the CEO and his direct reports. If the top team does not operate with trust, openness, cooperation, and effective communications, it is doubtful that the rest of the organization operates with these attributes. If the top team is not good at decision making and problem solving—if it does not reach a true consensus on company plans and objectives—then it is doubtful that the rest of the organization is pulling cooperatively in the right direction.

In fact, if the top team is in any way dysfunctional, that dysfunction does not dissipate as it permeates down through the organizational layers. To the contrary, the dysfunction becomes magnified; it increases in potency as it trickles from one level to another, similar to how small mountain streams come together to form a thunderous waterfall.

Not only does team-building have to start at the top, it also has to be based on the real issues within the team and the real problems that those issues generate in the organization. A good team-building consultant is able to show team members the connection between how they behave and how the organization as a whole behaves. If, for example, the top team is not good at agreeing on the key priorities facing the business, the consultant might show how lower levels of the organization are unclear on their key priorities.

The warning label on the team-building treatment is this: *Team-building disconnected from real business issues will not help a team address these issues.* Going whitewater rafting together, as some consultants recommend, may help members get to know each other, but it does not teach a team how to develop a business plan together. Learning about one another's personality type, as some consultants recommend, does not teach a team how to deal with an abusive boss who does not respect his people. Sending team members to sensitivity training, as some consultants recommend, does not teach the members how to expose a political shark on the team who keeps his dorsal fin hidden from the boss as he gnaws on the legs of his peers.

Perhaps the most important objective of a top management team-building effort is the development of an integrated corporate strategy and operating plan, one in which all of the team members have been able to contribute their views, their ideas, and their concerns and skepticism.

In too many cases, the development of the corporate strategy and operating plan has become a bureaucratic paper exercise controlled by the controller department. Typically, reams of paper containing millions of words, facts, and numbers are sent to the top team by each department head as part of the annual planning/budgeting process. Somehow, in some sort of mysterious executive ritual, the top team sorts through all the data like a powerful Cray computer and eventually communicates, in writing, back to the department heads what has been approved or modified. More often than not, the feedback from above focuses on the financial and budgetary numbers and only superficially addresses the key nonfinancial goals recommended by the department heads.

Predictably, what then happens later in the year is the discovery that the top team—and, hence, the rest of the organization—was not really in agreement on the strategy and operating plan, and had not really developed the top ten or fifteen goals, priorities, objectives, projects—or whatever the key, high-payoff things are called in the organization. Of course not! The backward, bureaucratic planning process runs counter to the clarity and agreement that are necessary in communicating the company's overall direction to the rest of the organization.

How would an effective senior team develop a strategy and operating plan in a spirit of teamwork, communications, and consensus? Easy. The team members would go offsite together for two to three days and, with or without the help of a team-building facilitator, reach agreement on the key priorities facing the business in the coming year. Team members would come to the meeting with a clear understanding of the key priorities of their own departments, ideally achieved beforehand through a consensus process with their own direct reports. In other words, the chief counsel might come to the meeting prepared to discuss the key priorities identified by his subordinates for the legal department, as well as the key priorities for the entire company.

The top team would leave the meeting at the end of two or three days with an agreement of what is going to be accomplished, by when, and by whom in the coming planning period. Then, and only then, the agreement would be used as a starting point for the formal budgetary and financial planning process controlled by the controller department. With such an approach to planning, the top team would perform the most important role of a top team; that is, giving direction to the organization.

So much space has been devoted to the subject of top management team-building and planning in this chapter because, without clarity and agreement at the top, other organizational treatments will have limited success. Let's turn to those other treatments and see why.

Employee Involvement

The concept of involving employees in decision making has many different definitions and has taken many different forms through the years, ranging from participative management, quality circles, employee empowerment, and self-managing teams. Employee involvement is an idea that was given birth to in the late 1960s and early 1970s, at which time it was largely ignored or given superficial support, primarily because American industry had no compelling reason back then to change the way it managed people. The economy was growing, global competition was just a faint murmur, and corporate management, with one of the most severe cases of hubris in history, mistakenly thought that the success of American companies was due to their leadership abilities and not to America's economic and military dominance after World War II, when Japan, Russia, and much of Europe lay in ruins and Britain's economic back had been broken, never to mend again, by the burdens of the war.

The faint murmur of global competition started to turn into a roar at the end of the 1970s, fueled by the quality revolution led by Japan. America's response? Quality circles.

Disappearing from the business scene just about as quickly as they appeared, quality circles resulted in marginal improvements in the quality of America's manufactured goods and marked improvements in the bottom lines of all the crackpot consulting firms that sprang up to pick the deep pockets of the Fortune 500. The tragedy of the quality circle movement was not that it failed; it was that the failure made managers cynical about the benefits of employee involvement, a cynicism that has taken almost a decade to overcome.

Quality circles were bound to fail because management let employees recommend improvements in operations but did not give them the power and authority to implement those recommendations. It was like a parent telling a sixteen-year-old, after a year of driver education classes, that he was trusted to take the family car on a date, only to have the parent jump in the back seat at the last moment as the teenager is pulling out of the driveway.

With the clarity of hindsight, it is now perfectly clear that quality cicles failed because the top management "teams" in those companies did not come together in an effective way to plan and direct the quality circle efforts. Instead of taking the time to work as a team in thinking through the organizational implications of quality circles, top management either willed that the circles be implemented or casually approved a circle program that bubbled up from below. In either case, no one did the hard work of changing the culture, the organization structure, the information systems, the reward programs, and the management practices needed to support a true quality circle culture. It is a safe bet that top management could not do so because they were buried in the millions of data generated by the financial and budgetary system, suffocating under an annual planning process that blocked out the fresh air of managing differently.

Because of the misuse of employee involvement, this popular treatment now comes with a warning label: *Do not use unless employees are going to be given the authority and power to make decisions. This treatment can be harmful to productivity and motivation if it is not supported by the top management team.*

Total Quality Management

The definitions of total quality management (TQM) are as varied as the number of TQM practitioners who make a living acting as consultants to businesses on quality.

Some practitioners define TQM as conformance to customer requirements. Some define it by such analytical tools as histograms, fishbone diagrams, and statistical process/quality control charts. Others define it by the continuous improvement of key business processes. Still others define it by an organizationwide culture that reinforces quality in everything that it does.

This book selects "all of the above" as the right definition. It believes that TQM is a nonhierarchical and nonbureaucratic culture, based on an operating philosophy of employee involvement, committed to meeting customer requirements through the continuous improvement of key business processes, as measured by a variety of analytical tools. Under this definition, TQM without employee involvement is a tool without a person; continuous improvement without measurement is unfocused activity; measurement without customer requirements is measurement for the sake of measurement. And, most important, TQM built on a foundation of hierarchy and bureaucracy is a program that will not stand the test of time.

Chapter 9 described the dandelion-free world of Mars, where quality was attained long before the techniques of TQM became popular, long before employee involvement became the newest way of managing people, and long before "customer requirements" became part of the business lexicon. The secret to Mars' success is its quality culture—its unique way of developing managers, of rewarding its people, of measuring its business.

At Mars, quality is congruent with the values, beliefs, philosophies, and behaviors of its senior managers, all of whom "walk the talk" and "practice what they preach," most of whom have grown up in the Mars world and understand no other way of operating. At Mars, quality is not a program, an event, a project, or hollow words; rather, it is a way of life, a corporate religion, and an unrelenting principle to be followed by everyone. At Mars, a true quality culture came before TQM and not the other way around.

The world of Mars has read the warning label on the TQM treatment, the one that says: *Do not apply TQM techniques without also creating a quality culture.*

Team Organizations

Team organizations are an outgrowth of the employee involvement and TQM movement. They are replacing the traditional command-and-control, functional-based structures found in hierarchical organizations. These new organizational forms have two shapes.

The first shape is the self-managing work team. Usually comprised of a natural work group (for example, the employees in a shipping department), the teams do not have a traditional supervisor. Rather, they manage their own work schedule, their own quality, their own safety program, and sometimes, their own hiring, firing, and performance reviews—all under guidelines and measurements set by the organization.

The second shape is the cross-functional team, which is usually comprised of employees from various functional areas (for example, finance, manufacturing, sales, distribution). The team can be a temporary team established to complete a given project, or it can be a permanent team with an ongoing mission to cross the boundaries of functional departments. An example of a permanent team would be a customer order team whose mission would be to process customer orders in the most efficient and time-sensitive way possible. The team might require membership from MIS, finance, distribution, and customer service.

The power of teams is that they can break through the functional walls that surround departments in a traditional organization. Communications among team members is lateral and unfiltered, versus the communications in a hierarchical organization that must go up and down the pyramid, being second-guessed and filtered every step of the way.

The team treatment comes with this warning on its label: *This treatment will have limited success if team members are rewarded for individual effort instead of team results.*

Business Process Re-engineering

Ah, the newest buzzword, the newest prescription to save American industry, the newest panacea touted by the newest consulting firms. The warning label on this treatment is clear: *Only use under the supervision of a skilled practitioner with a proven track record of success. Beware of intelligent-sounding college professors who have never worked in a business organization.*

Business process re-engineering is done on both a macro level and a micro level. On a macro level, it entails the radical redesign of work in organizations, primarily building an organization around processes instead of functional departments. It is the cross-functional team approach carried to its logical extension.

A functional organization might have the standard departments of manufacturing, sales and marketing, research and development, purchasing, finance, legal, MIS, human resources, and so on. An organization built on key business processes, on the other hand, might be organized into the processes of generating and fulfilling customer orders, procuring raw materials, transforming raw materials into finished products, developing new products, and so on.

On a micro level, business process re-engineering takes apart a key business process, improves it, and puts it back together again—all in the interest of reducing cycle times, increasing responsiveness, lowering processing costs, and improving accuracy. An example might be the processing of invoices, which in most organizations is a paper-intensive process with many checks and balances from start to finish. Business process re-engineering would look for opportunities to reduce the number of steps in the process, the amount of paperwork, and the degree of checks and balances. Usually, business process re-engineering does this through integrated computer systems that effectively tie the various internal departments together with real-time data and are linked to the external customer through an electronic data interface. Paper invoices have all but disappeared in companies that have used re-engineering to improve the invoicing process.

Starting at the Top

This book was not written to start a new fad. It was written to solve an old problem, one that has plagued human organizations since the birth of the nation-state, a problem that is keeping business organizations from realizing all the potential gains from total quality management, employee involvement, team structures, and business process re-engineering.

The problem is, of course, bureaucracy. And the problem with the problem is that it cannot be solved without substantial change, which must start from the top where the roots of bureaucracy are deep and many. Those in power cannot lay the blame for the problem on others. They have to be tough enough and confident enough to look in the mirror and say that the problem starts with themselves, not with lower-level functionaries.

The solution also starts at the top. If the top wants the organization to be nonbureaucratic, nimble, willing to change, and lean and mean, then the top has to be nonbureaucratic, nimble, willing to change, and lean and mean. Double-standards will not work. The top cannot have plush surroundings, private secretaries, limousines, executive dining rooms, and pathological power and control needs, and, at the same time, expect the lower levels of the organization to be concerned about costs, efficiency, productivity, and teamwork.

The astute chief executive must "cultivate a visceral hatred of bureaucracy,"[1] to quote Jack Welch of General Electric.

He must also have an understanding of the root causes of bureaucracy and an effective way of removing those root causes. This book has attempted to provide both the understanding and the methodology.

And this section of the book concludes with a "Grim Fairy

Tale" that is being faxed around the country by employees of corporate America. The author of the masterpiece is unknown:

A GRIM FAIRY TALE

Once upon a time, an American automobile company and a Japanese auto company decided to have a competitive boat race on the Detroit River. Both teams practiced hard and long to reach their peak performance. On the big day, they were as ready as they could be.

The Japanese team won by a mile.

Afterward, the American team became discouraged by the loss and their morale sagged. Corporate management decided that the reason for the crushing defeat had to be found. A Continuous Measurable Improvement Team of executives was set up to investigate the problem and to recommend appropriate corrective action.

Their conclusion: The problem was that the Japanese team had eight people rowing and one person steering, whereas the American team had one person rowing and eight people steering. The American Corporate Steering Committee immediately hired a consulting firm to do a study on the management structure.

After some time and billions of dollars, the consulting firm concluded that "too many people were steering and not enough rowing." To prevent losing to the Japanese again next year, the management structure was changed to "four steering managers, three area steering managers, and one staff steering manager," and a new performance system for the person rowing the boat to give more incentive to work harder and become a six-sigma performer. "We must give him empowerment and enrichment. That ought to do it."

The next year the Japanese team won by two miles.

The American corporation laid off the rower for poor performance, sold all of the paddles, canceled all capital investments for new equipment, halted development of a new canoe, awarded high-performance awards to the consulting firm, and distributed the money saved as bonuses to the senior executives.

Note

1. GE Shareholder Meeting, April 22, 1992.

III
Case Studies

Case One

The Insurance Policy

"The Insurance Policy" is a short case in how *not* to stop the growth of dandelions. It is in sharp contrast to the next case, "The Sales Bag," which demonstrates the right way of killing the bureaucratic weed using the bottom-up and outside-in approach outlined in Part II.

"The Insurance Policy" takes place twenty years ago in the mid-1970s; "The Sales Bag," in the mid-1980s. Ironically, "The Insurance Policy" is more contemporary than "The Sales Bag" because it still represents the common way that companies approach the twin problems of hierarchy and bureaucracy. The approach in "The Sales Bag" was an anomaly in 1985 and would still be an anomaly today.

"The Insurance Policy" is based on Zurich-American Insurance Company, the United States subsidiary of the huge, Swiss-owned, multinational Zurich Insurance Group, which underwrites all the major lines of insurance.

Like many insurance companies, Zurich-American is selling its policies through independent insurance agents and brokers. It has a headquarters operation in Chicago and twenty-five branch offices in key cities across the United States. Headquarters has the standard functions of underwriting, claims, loss control, investments, marketing, MIS, accounting, audits, human resources, and training. Most of these functions are replicated in the branches, where authority levels are less than in headquarters, meaning that underwriting decisions and claim settlements over certain risk exposures or dollar limits have to be sent to headquarters for review and approval.

Zurich-American's operating style and organization structure reflect the copycat mentality of the insurance industry, whereby all similarly sized companies are operated and organized largely the same way, even to the extent of employees having virtually identical job titles and pay levels.

Zurich-American has a new president. He is a mover and shaker from CNA, a considerably larger company located down the street from Zurich-American's headquarters in the Chicago Loop. He has brought his young strategic planning vice-president along with him.

One of the first decisions of the new president and his strategic planning vice-president is to mimic the organizational structure of their last company. They want to decentralize Zurich-American and move decision making closer to the customers (the independent agents) by setting up regional, or zone, offices.

The offices would include most of the functions found at headquarters and are to be headed up by zone vice-presidents. Four offices would be established: Chicago; Jackson, Mississippi; Moorestown, New Jersey; and Fresno, California—locations picked for their proximity to the branches in their respective regions (zones) and for the good work ethic of the local population. Each zone office would have one-fourth of the total number of branch offices reporting to it.

The president dictates that the offices will be up and running in record time. Thousands of details and decisions are compressed unrealistically: expensive facilities are built or leased, computer systems designed and installed, forms redesigned and printed, records boxed and shipped, people hired, people promoted, people transferred, and people trained. Confusion reigns. Customer service deteriorates. Accountability and authority levels become blurred.

One would expect the headquarters operation to shrink as decisions are pushed downward to the new zone offices. A reasonable but wrong expectation.

Because the new organization was designed by headquarters executives, headquarters is not about to relinquish much authority or positions to the zone offices. Predictably, the zone offices, unable to get authority or positions from above, begin stealing them from the only available source—from below, from the branch offices.

The people closest to the customers in the branch offices suddenly find themselves with two headquarters hierarchies above them. If they want to hire or fire someone, they now have to get approval from the zone human resources department, which, in turn, has to get approval from the headquarters human resources department. If they want to underwrite a casualty policy for a large factory, they now have to go through two levels of approval instead of the one level of the past.

Naturally, the zone offices have their jobs evaluated higher than those in the branches, resulting in the better people transferring to the higher-paid zone jobs, from which they begin to second-guess their old associates in the branches.

Dandelions have sprung up all over the place. There are new procedures, new policies, new controls, new overhead, new politicking and jockeying for position. The freedom and flexibility of the branch offices are slowly sinking into a swamp of red tape by the weight of the new superstructure above them.

To their credit, the astute Swiss business leaders back in Zurich see the bureaucracy created by the zone concept. They quickly install a new president from their Canadian subsidiary and begin to dismantle much of the zone offices. Moving vans begin to crisscross the country, relocating employees and their families. Many management-level zone-office employees, not wanting to return to a lowly branch position, begin to send out their resumes.

How many millions were wasted on this ill-conceived top-down and inside-out approach to reorganization? A bunch. What would the organization have looked like if it had been designed from the bottom-up and outside-in? Hard to say, but for sure it would not have resulted in the additional bureaucracy and hierarchy that were hatched by the president and his strategic planning vice-president in the rarified air of corporate headquarters.

"The Insurance Policy" is really a case of centralized decentralization, in which a well-intentioned attempt at decentralizing authority had the opposite result, primarily because the effort was planned through the eyes at the top of the pyramid instead of those at the bottom. Centralization in the guise of decentralization happens all the time, usually when another layer of management is inserted into an organization. Even if the other layer is just one person, like a group vice-president, the inevitable result is more bureaucracy, not less; more interference, not less; more politics, not less.

Now let's return to the planet Mars.

Case Two

The Sales Bag

It is the mid-1980s. At $1.5 billion in sales, M&M/Mars is the largest operating unit in the Mars universe. It manufactures and markets all of the candy products for Mars in the United States. Sister units manufacture and sell other products domestically and internationally.

Like other food manufacturers in the consumer products industry, M&M/Mars has two types of customers. One, the consumer, is the ultimate purchaser of the company's products. The other, called the trade, is the thousands of supermarkets, convenience stores, gas stations, vending machine companies, newsstands, and theaters that sell the products to the ultimate consumer.

In the world of Mars, the ultimate consumer has always been king. The long-held belief is that quality products, providing good value to the consumer, will sell themselves without having to pay undue attention to the trade. Accordingly, the sales department, which is responsible for selling to the trade, is rather low on the totem pole of status and influence at Mars. Highest on the pole is manufacturing, since that is where product quality begins and ends. Next highest is marketing, which, like many consumer products marketing departments, is staffed with product managers who hold MBAs from the top business schools.

Marketing is responsible for consumer advertising (television, radio, print), pricing, and packaging design. It is also responsible for two types of promotions: (1) trade promotions that give discounts to the trade for pushing certain brands and package sizes; and (2) consumer promotions that give discounts to the consumer, such as cents-off coupons.

Trade promotions are a never-ending cycle of futility for consumer products companies. Constantly giving various types of discounts to the trade, the promotions only result in temporary blips in revenues that, after the promotions have run their course and the trade has filled its warehouses with promoted product, fall back below where they would have been without the promotions. But because every company in the industry relies on promo-

tions for achieving short-term revenue goals, every company must go along with the practice as a defensive measure.

In theory, consumer products marketing departments have the additional responsibility of coordinating the activities of sales and manufacturing to achieve the best profit margins. In practice, the departments have a difficult time of doing this well. Like many companies, M&M/Mars has tried to improve coordination by having the sales department report to the marketing department, where few of the hotshot MBAs have ever worked in sales.

Due to the insistence of the owners to cut overhead and bureaucracy, M&M/Mars has undertaken a companywide study of its organization, using the bottom-up and outside-in approach outlined in Chapter 11. An organization effectiveness consultant is working with a full-time project team consisting of key people from finance, distribution, sales, marketing, human resources, and manufacturing.

Some of the early findings of the team have startled the senior staff, particularly the findings from the sales department. To understand the findings, let's digress for a moment and look at how the sales department is organized at the time.

The basic organization consists of the headquarters functions of sales administration and national accounts, and the field structure of 4 sales regions, 16 districts, and 60 units. It looks like this:

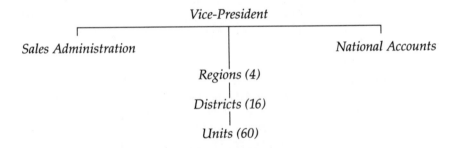

Vice-President

Sales Administration   *National Accounts*

Regions (4)

Districts (16)

Units (60)

The organization of the 60 units is key, since they are the frontline interface with the trade customers:

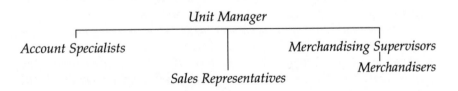

Unit Manager

Account Specialists   *Merchandising Supervisors*

Merchandisers

Sales Representatives

Nationwide, there are approximately 400 sales representatives, 60 merchandising supervisors, and 100 account specialists. In addition, there are about 300 merchandisers, who, as part-time employees, work 20 hours per week.

It is the job of the sales representative to call on retail stores (supermarkets, for example) and small headquarter accounts in a defined territory. The merchandising supervisors are responsible for hiring, training, and supervising the part-time merchandisers, whose job it is to assist the sales representatives at the retail level in rotating stock and keeping shelves and displays in the proper order. The account specialists call on the headquarters of the larger retailers within the unit's geography. Merchandising supervisors and account specialists are higher paid than sales representatives.

Returning to the findings of the organization project team, let's see some of the bitter pills that the team has presented to the senior staff of M&M/ Mars.

One pill is the opinion of the trade about customer service. Of particular concern is the way that the company executes trade and consumer promotions. Example after example has been relayed to the project team of product not being available after promotions had been sold to the trade by the sales force. This problem is particularly irksome to the trade because the trade ends up with its own customer relations problems when it advertises a price discount and then does not have the product available to its customers.

The sales force is just as irked, for it has become the punching bag for the trade's frustrations. Forced to sell promotions without the necessary inventory in stock, the sales force has become demoralized, frustrated, and cynical. The problem has become so serious that a training video has been developed to teach the sales force how to overcome the distrust of the trade about product availability.

Worse yet, elaborate coordination mechanisms have been developed at headquarters in a feeble attempt to solve the problem. The sales administration function, for example, has been given the impossible task of reviewing all promotions and directives from marketing to the field sales force, but without being given the authority to stop anything. And the production planning department, which reports to finance, has the "mission impossible" of coordinating the volume projections of marketing with the sales forecasts of sales and with the production scheduling of manufacturing. Accountability for accurate forecasting and scheduling have become so blurred that no one is held accountable when product is not available for promotions.

The next bitter pill is the news that the sales force is being buried in an avalanche of memos, forms, information requests, and outdated reports from headquarters. Not believed at first, the news is finally driven home by the project team when it walks into a senior staff meeting with a handtruck full of the paper being dumped on the sales force by the rest of the company.

Another pill is just as big and just as bitter. It is the perspective of the sales representatives on the effectiveness of the unit organization. As expressed by the sale representatives, there are a number of serious problems with the structure.

The first is the fact that the part-time merchandisers, who support the sales representatives by helping out in retail stores, do not report to the sales representatives. Therefore, if the sales representative needs to get something done, he must go up the chain-of-command to his boss, the unit manager, who then goes to the merchandising supervisor, who finally contacts the appropriate merchandiser. The communication flow looks like this:

The flow is reversed if a merchandiser determines that something in a store needs the attention of a sales representative.

A complicating factor is that the responsibility for recruiting merchandisers resides with the merchandising supervisor, who gets help in this from the human resources staff at headquarters. The sales representatives are not pleased with the time it takes to fill openings or with the quality of some of the hires.

An additional complicaing factor is that the performance evaluations of merchandisers are, of course, done by the merchandising supervisors, although the sales representatives are in the best position to know how a merchandiser has performed.

Another serious problem with the unit organization is the position of account specialist, which is a better-paid position than the sales representative. The job of the account specialist is to call on the larger headquarters accounts in the unit's geography, selling promotions, product, and programs that the headquarter accounts will pass on to their retail stores, which is the domain of the sale representatives.

As seen by the sales representatives, and as documented by the project team, this arrangement is far from efficient or responsive to customer needs. For one thing, the communication process between sales representatives and account specialists is almost as cumbersome as that between sales representatives and merchandisers. Again, communications goes from the sales representative, up the chain-of-command to the unit managers, and then down to the account specialist. For another, the sales representative no longer feels accountable for the performance of his sales territory because the account specialist, who no longer works at the retail level, is making decisions that affect pricing and sales volume at the retail level. And, speaking with emotion, the sales representatives feel that the account specialists do not have to work very hard for their higher pay.

After following information flows and business processes from the customer, through the sales representative, and up the organization to the corporate headquarters of M&M/Mars, the project team has summarized the key issues affecting the performance of the sales force. They are:

1. Blurred Accountability for Trade Promotions. *A great deal of ambiguity exists as to which department is accountable for the success or failure of trade promotions. Is it marketing? Production scheduling? Sales administration? Field sales? As long as the ambiguity exists, the project team feels that promotion performance in the eyes of the trade customers will continue to be poor, regardless of how many control mechanisms or measurements are implemented to try to deal with the problem.*

2. Blurred Accountability for Merchandising. *It is unclear who is responsible for retail store conditions. Is it the sales representative? The merchandising supervisor? The merchandiser?*

3. Blurred Accountability for Retail Sales Volume. *Does the accountability for achieving retail sales volume goals reside with the sales representative or with the account specialist?*

4. Blurred Accountability for Merchandiser Performance. *Who is accountable for the recruitment, selection, training, and evaluation of the part-time merchandisers? Corporate human resources? Merchandising supervisors? Sales representatives?*

Applying the root removal principles of Chapter 11, the project team has developed the following recommendations to deal with the issues listed above:

1. Whole Jobs. *The sales representatives should be given as much planning, controlling, and doing responsibility as they can handle. To the extent possible, they should be viewed as mini-general managers of their territories, responsible for anything that goes on within their geographic boundaries, including calling on the headquarter accounts currently being covered by the account specialists.*

2. Unit Structure. *In support of the above, the jobs of merchandising supervisor and account specialist should be eliminated. Merchandisers should report to sales representatives, who, instead of the merchandising supervisors, should recruit, train, supervise, and evaluate the merchandisers: The new structure should look like this:*

Unit Manager

|

Sales Representatives

|

Merchandisers

3. Pay Levels. *Because the new unit structure would eliminate the jobs of the merchandising supervisors and account specialists, the incumbents in those jobs should be given sales representative positions at their current higher-pay levels, as long as their performance warrants the higher pay. Lower-paid sales representatives should then be able to move up to the higher-pay level over time if they demonstrate the requisite performance and competence. Under this arrangement, sales representatives could be promoted without having to move up the hierarchy.*

4. Top Structure. *The sales department should be taken from under the marketing department and report directly to the M&M/Mars president, where it would have equal power with marketing and manufacturing, thus being able to control the flow of trade promotions and paperwork to the people in the field. Moreover, the role of the production planning department should be reduced, because sales, marketing, and manufacturing should work as a team in agreeing on sales forecasts and production targets.*

5. Trade Promotions. *When ready, the sales department should be given the responsibility and budget for planning, designing, and executing trade promotions, instead of the current system of having the planning and designing done in marketing.*

The strongest objections to these proposals come from three places: the marketing department, which thinks that sales people are not sufficiently knowledgeable of marketing to take over trade promotions; the human resources department, which feels that the company will be sued for discrimination and sexual harassment if sales representatives with no supervisory experience are asked to supervise merchandisers; and the finance department, which feels that chaos will occur if the power of the production planning department is reduced.

Surprisingly, many of the account specialists and merchandising supervisors see the value in the proposed structure and are anxious to return to meaningful work at the sales representative level, especially when they find out that there will be no reduction in pay and that they will be fully responsible for their own territories.

The sales vice-president, a fairly new employee of M&M/Mars, supports the recommendations of the project team. Of more importance is the strong support of the president, a very influential executive within Mars who is due to retire soon. He adopts virtually all of the task force recommendations, not only those listed above, but the hundreds of others that were made for improving the structures, information flows, and business processes in the other parts of the company.

Results are dramatic. The impact of having 35 percent more sales representatives (the 150 or so ex-merchandising supervisors and account specialists) at the retail level can be seen almost immediately in market share increases—at no additional cost to the company. Trade promotion problems are sharply reduced, thus bringing about a marked improvement in trade relations. Communications and cooperation between sales representatives and merchandisers are significantly better and easier. Unnecessary paperwork and red tape are eliminated.

The changes described in "The Sales Bag" case were certainly not the final changes at M&M/Mars. Subsequent changes in structure and operations were to start coming in rapid succession due to significant changes in the food industry, including the widespread use of optical scanners that gave the trade quick feedback on the buying habits of its consumers; the consolidation of food manufacturers through leveraged buyouts that created huge competing sales forces; the reliance on electronic data interchange between manufacturers and retailers to manage inventory levels; and the increased use of voice mail and laptop computers that made communications easier between employees in the field.

All of these changes demonstrate that dandelion removal is a never-ending process. The vigilant manager, just like the vigilant homeowner, must be constantly on guard against changes in the outside environment that are conducive to the growth of dandelions. Just because an organization is nonbureaucratic today does not mean that it will be nonbureaucratic tomorrow. One only hopes that Mars remains vigilant and does not allow dandelions to take root.

Final Note

I am both encouraged and discouraged from what I learned in researching and writing this book.

Encouragement certainly comes from all the companies that are sincerely trying to create a culture of total quality, free of bureaucracy and focused on the requirements of the customer. Thank goodness that companies like Mars, Vi-Jon, and Sigma-Aldrich are not isolated examples.

Unfortunately, there are so many other companies that still don't get it. In the course of interviewing scores of executives and employees, plus the firsthand experience of working at the top of a variety of industries, I found many reasons for being discouraged about the state of affairs in American business.

Perhaps the most discouraging aspect of writing this book was entering the inner sanctums of corporate America to interview senior executives. Making it through the phalanx of public relations personnel, I would find myself in the executive suite of offices, where the sounds of silence would emanate from the plush carpet; where the executive secretaries would stand guard outside the imperial offices, one for each executive; where the lack of hustle and bustle was embarrassingly noticeable; and where the hushed atmosphere reminded me of an empty church on Friday night. What a contrast to the noisy, animated, and hurried atmosphere of Mars or Sigma-Aldrich!

My discouragement goes beyond the executive suite. It extends to the Wall Street investment community and much of the business media. It seemed that if either institution branded a company as well-run, I was almost certain to find a model of bureaucracy and hierarchy.

As an example, the June 17, 1991, issue of *Fortune* magazine carried a front-page story called "Bureaucracy Busters." It
cited the chairman of a multibillion-dollar company and his
Harvard consultant as examples of bureaucracy busters. It just
so happens that I interviewed with a number of executives and
managers from an operating division of that company. What
did I find? A high degree of frustration with the bureaucracy
at headquarters, with the rapid growth of the headquarters
staff, and with the new Taj Mahal headquarters building and
its brick driveways and executive dining room.

Could it be that the investment community and business
press evaluate a company by quarterly results and by the
amount of glass and marble at headquarters instead of the
efficiency, productivity, cleanliness, quality, safety, and morale
found in the back rooms and factories? If so, a well-run company like Mars is in trouble if it ever goes public and opens
itself up to the myopic eyes of Wall Street analysts and business
journalists.

The realization has slowly come to this slow learner that
much of what is viewed as good management in high-flying
companies is simply the result of decisions, innovations, strategies, and products developed by earlier generations of management, sometimes going all the way back to the entrepreneurial founder. Some of these companies are so rich in
products, market share, consumer franchises, and cash flow
that they would have a forward momentum regardless of
whom is at the helm.

Breaking the iron laws of bureaucracy is going to be difficult in these rich organizations, which are headed up by heirs
to the throne who hold court in their imperial headquarters
surrounded by staff courtiers. The only hope for positive
change in those fiefs is for the ruler to be overthrown when his
kingdom inevitably loses touch with reality—that is, with the
peasants at the bottom of the kingdom and, hence, with the
marketplace. It's too bad, though, that when the imperial ruler
is deposed, he is given a jewel of a severance package while
the peasants are left with a bankrupt treasury.

The discouragement is not limited to large companies.
Sadly, many smaller companies were found to be aggressively

pursuing total quality management programs at the expense of fixing serious problems within their organizations, thus expending time and energy on a low-priority initiative with little payoff. One $40 million company with a serious inventory control problem had put the problem aside to spend $80,000 on an introductory quality course. Another company, a sixty-employee insurance agency, was starting a TQM program although it had serious revenue and profit problems and was lacking a business plan on how to turn the business around. Customers calling into the agency could not get through to employees because they were attending quality training. Still another company was conducting safety training for office workers, although the risk of accidents in the office was infinitesimal, because "safety training is one of the Baldrige Award criteria."

In a very real sense, these well-intentioned companies have created bureaucracy through their TQM efforts by generating TQM activity that adds no value to the enterprise. They are truly victims of the iron laws of bureaucracy.

Notwithstanding all the discouragement, I am feeling much more optimistic than pessimistic, primarily because so many people reviewed the manuscript to this book and wanted to send anonymous copies to the bureaucrats in their companies, along with dead dandelions wrapped in newspaper, just like the Mafia does with dead fish, warning that their days may be numbered. And more and more requests are coming in for help in eliminating bureaucracy, even from the last bastion of bureaucracy—corporate headquarters.

Those people are right. The days of the bureaucrat are indeed numbered.

Index